150

PASTA
recipes

INSPIRED IDEAS FOR
EVERYDAY COOKING

CONTENTS

INTRODUCTION

Pasta is a superb and savvy storecupboard staple as it can be used to create a vast variety of delicious dishes, from no-fuss midweek meals to more elaborate eats. An extensive range of both dried and fresh pasta is readily available, including white and wholewheat varieties, plus speciality pasta like gluten-free, and for pasta pros in the know, making your own pasta at home is very satisfying.

Pasta is a versatile ingredient and is perfect for creating fast and fabulous family meals. You'll soon build up a repertoire of enticing dishes with this comprehensive collection of practical pasta dishes, many of which can be rustled up in minutes so are sure to earn a regular slot at the table.

We include popular pasta dishes to suit any occasion, including flavourful fuss-free suppers for the family to feast on, plus inspirational dishes ideal for

special occasions. Soups and salads all feature, plus gnocchi, gratins, lasagnes and other top bakes too, so revolutionize your weeknight cooking with these fantastic pasta dishes.

Different types of pasta feature throughout, including shapes such as fusilli, penne, rigatoni, conchiglie, macaroni, farfalle, orzo and ziti, as well as long varieties like spaghetti, tagliatelle, linguine, pappardelle and fettuccine, ensuring you have plenty of choice when selecting recipes. Flavour-packed filled pasta like ravioli, tortellini and cannelloni, also take centre stage in some delicious dishes.

We begin with a tempting choice of vegetable and dairy dishes which includes classics like Pasta all'Arrabbiata and Macaroni Cheese, plus other delights such as Creamy Pappardelle & Broccoli, Wild Mushroom Fusilli and Fettuccine All'Alfredo.

Next up we focus on mouth-watering meat-based recipes featuring everyday favourites like Spaghetti Carbonara, Spaghetti Bolognese and Pepperoni Pasta. More deluxe, sumptuous meaty marvels include Farfalle with Gorgonzola & Ham, Pasta & Pork in Cream Sauce and Tagliatelle with Lamb.

A super selection of poultry-based dishes is next, promising plenty of appealing weeknight pleasers, including soups, salads, medleys and meatballs. Opt for choices like Italian Chicken Spirals and Turkey Pasta Pesto, or tongue-tingling temptations like Spicy Chicken Pasta, Pasta with Harissa Turkey Meatballs or Pasta with Chilli Barbecue Sauce.

For fish and seafood lovers, our appealing assortment of fabulous dishes includes Sea Bass with Olive Sauce, Salad Niçoise and Fettuccine with Lemon Pepper Seafood. For easy entertaining, choose Sicilian Swordfish Pasta, Tagliatelle with Smoked Salmon & Rocket or Farfallini Buttered Lobster.

A final selection of full-on-flavour filled and baked pasta dishes features ever-popular bakes like Chicken & Leek Lasagne and Tuna Pasta Bake, or enjoy Chicken & Wild Mushroom Cannelloni or Steak & Pasta Bites.

Quantities

For a main meal (using plain or stuffed pasta), allow 85–115 g (3–4 oz) dried pasta or 115–140 g (4–5 oz) fresh pasta per person.

Cooking

Cook pasta in a large pan of salted, boiling water. Add pasta to the boiling water, stir to separate, return to the boil and time from this point. Leave pan partially covered; stir pasta occasionally. Cook pasta until al dente (just tender but still firm to the bite), drain thoroughly and serve promptly. If serving pasta cold (in a salad), rinse under cold running water; drain well.

Follow the cooking times on the packet. As a rough guide, dried unfilled pasta takes 8–12 minutes to cook; dried filled pasta sometimes slightly longer. Fresh unfilled and filled pasta (and home-made pasta) takes 1–4 minutes to cook.

Storage

Store dried pasta in an airtight container in a cool, dry cupboard; it should keep for many months (check best-before date). Keep shop-bought fresh pasta sealed in the refrigerator; it has a much shorter shelf-life (check use-by date). Keep home-made pasta in the refrigerator; use within 1–2 days.

VEGETABLES & DAIRY

HEARTY BEAN & PASTA SOUP

Serves: 4　　　　**Prep: 15 mins**　　　　**Cook: 45 mins**

Ingredients

4 tbsp olive oil

1 onion, finely chopped

1 celery stick, chopped

1 carrot, diced

1 bay leaf

1.2 litres/2 pints low-salt vegetable stock

400 g/14 oz canned chopped tomatoes

175 g/6 oz dried pasta shapes, such as farfalle, shells or twists

400 g/14 oz canned cannellini beans, drained and rinsed

200 g/7 oz spinach or chard, thick stalks removed and shredded

salt and pepper

40 g/1½ oz Parmesan cheese, finely grated, to serve

Method

1 Heat the olive oil in a large, heavy-based saucepan. Add the onion, celery and carrot and cook over a medium heat for 8–10 minutes, stirring occasionally, until the vegetables slightly soften. Add the bay leaf, stock and tomatoes, then bring to the boil.

2 Reduce the heat, cover and simmer for 15 minutes, or until the vegetables are just tender. Add the pasta and beans, then bring the soup back to the boil and cook for 10 minutes, until the pasta is tender but still firm to the bite.

3 Stir occasionally to prevent the pasta sticking to the bottom of the pan and burning. Season to taste with salt and pepper, add the spinach and cook for a further 2 minutes, or until tender. Ladle the soup into warmed bowls and serve with Parmesan cheese.

★ Variation

For an even more colourful alternative, try replacing the cannellini beans with borlotti or red kidney beans.

ORZO & VEGETABLE SOUP

Serves: 2   **Prep: 10–15 mins**   **Cook: 20 mins**

Ingredients

1 tbsp olive oil

1 bunch spring onions, finely chopped

850 ml/1½ pints vegetable stock

100 g/3½ oz dried orzo

175 g/6 oz roasted red peppers, drained and sliced

100 g/3½ oz French green beans, trimmed and cut into short lengths

85 g/3 oz spinach, de-stemmed and roughly chopped

salt and pepper

Parmesan cheese shavings, to serve

extra virgin olive oil, to serve

Method

1 Heat the oil in a saucepan over medium–high heat, add the spring onions and sauté for 2–3 minutes, or until starting to soften.

2 Add the stock and orzo and bring to the boil. Season to taste with salt and pepper, then cover and simmer for 8 minutes.

3 Add the peppers, beans and spinach and cook for a further 2–3 minutes, then taste and adjust the seasoning, if necessary. Serve with Parmesan cheese shavings and a drizzle of olive oil.

ROASTED TOMATO WHOLEWHEAT PASTA SALAD

Serves: 4

Prep: 20–25 mins
plus cooling

Cook: 40–45 mins

Ingredients

600 g/1 lb 5 oz tomatoes in various colours and sizes, halved

2 garlic cloves, finely chopped

6 tbsp olive oil

225 g/8 oz dried wholewheat pasta, such as mafalda corta or quills

85 g/3 oz baby spinach

salt and pepper

Spinach pesto

50 g/1¾ oz fresh basil, plus extra leaves to garnish

25 g/1 oz pine nuts

25 g/1 oz Parmesan cheese, finely grated, plus Parmesan shavings to garnish

Method

1 Preheat the oven to 160°C/325°F/Gas Mark 3. Put the tomatoes in a roasting tin, cut side up, sprinkle with the garlic and 2 tablespoons of olive oil and season well with salt and pepper. Roast for 40–45 minutes, or until softened and just beginning to brown. Leave to cool, then chop up any larger ones.

2 Meanwhile, put the pasta in a large saucepan of boiling water. Bring back to the boil, cover and simmer according to the packet instructions, until just tender. Drain into a colander, rinse with cold water, then drain again.

3 To make the pesto, put all the ingredients in a blender, add 25 g/1 oz baby spinach and the remaining 4 tablespoons of olive oil and whizz until smooth. Season lightly with salt and pepper.

4 Put the pasta and pesto in a salad bowl, toss together, then add the remaining spinach and toss again briefly. Add the tomatoes and any pan juices and toss gently. Garnish with the Parmesan shavings and basil leaves and serve.

PASTA WITH TOMATO & BASIL SAUCE

Serves: 4   **Prep: 20–25 mins**   **Cook: 40 mins**

Ingredients

2 fresh rosemary sprigs

2 garlic cloves, unpeeled

450 g/1 lb tomatoes, halved

1 tbsp olive oil

1 tbsp sun-dried tomato purée

12 fresh basil leaves, plus extra to garnish

675 g/1 lb 8 oz fresh farfalle or 350 g/12 oz dried farfalle

salt and pepper

Method

1 Place the rosemary, garlic and tomatoes, skin side up, in a shallow roasting tin.

2 Preheat the grill to medium. Drizzle with the oil and cook under the preheated grill for 20 minutes, or until the tomato skins are slightly charred.

3 Peel the skin from the tomatoes. Roughly chop the tomato flesh and place in a saucepan. Squeeze the pulp from the garlic cloves and mix with the tomato flesh and sun-dried tomato purée.

4 Roughly tear the fresh basil leaves into smaller pieces and then stir them into the sauce. Season with a little salt and pepper to taste.

5 Place a saucepan of lightly salted water over a high heat and bring to the boil. Add the farfalle, bring back to the boil and cook for 10 minutes, or until tender but still firm to the bite.

6 Gently heat the tomato and basil sauce. Transfer the farfalle to serving plates and serve with the tomato sauce over the top. Garnish with the basil.

PASTA
ALL'ARRABBIATA

Serves: 4   **Prep: 20 mins**   **Cook: 30 mins**

Ingredients

150 ml/5 fl oz dry white wine

1 tbsp sun-dried
tomato purée

2 fresh red chillies

2 garlic cloves,
finely chopped

4 tbsp chopped fresh
flat-leaf parsley

400 g/14 oz dried penne

salt and pepper

fresh pecorino cheese
shavings, to garnish

Sugocasa

5 tbsp extra virgin olive oil

450 g/1 lb plum
tomatoes, chopped

salt and pepper

Method

1 To make the sugocasa, heat the oil in a frying
pan over a high heat until almost smoking. Add
the tomatoes and cook, stirring frequently, for
2–3 minutes.

2 Reduce the heat to low and cook for about
20 minutes. Season to taste with salt and
pepper. Using a wooden spoon, press through
a non-metallic sieve into a saucepan.

3 Add the wine, tomato purée, whole chillies and
garlic to the pan and bring to the boil. Reduce
the heat and simmer gently for 10 minutes,
then remove the chillies. Check and adjust the
seasoning, adding the chillies back in for a hotter
sauce, then stir in half the parsley.

4 Meanwhile, bring a large saucepan of lightly
salted water to the boil. Add the pasta, bring
back to the boil and cook for 8–10 minutes,
or until tender but still firm to the bite. Add the
sauce to the pasta and toss to coat.

5 Sprinkle with the remaining parsley, garnish with
cheese shavings and serve immediately.

VEGETABLES & DAIRY

SPAGHETTI ALLA NORMA

Serves: 4   **Prep: 20 mins**   **Cook: 30 mins**

Ingredients

175 ml/6 fl oz olive oil

500 g/1 lb 2 oz plum tomatoes, peeled and chopped

1 garlic clove, chopped

350 g/12 oz aubergines, diced

400 g/14 oz dried spaghetti

½ bunch fresh basil, torn

115 g/4 oz freshly grated pecorino cheese

salt and pepper

Method

1 Heat 4 tablespoons of the oil in a large saucepan. Add the tomatoes and garlic, season to taste with salt and pepper, cover and cook over a low heat, stirring occasionally, for 25 minutes.

2 Meanwhile, heat the remaining oil in a heavy-based frying pan. Add the aubergines and cook, stirring occasionally, for 5 minutes, until evenly golden brown. Remove with a slotted spoon and drain on kitchen paper.

3 Bring a large, heavy-based saucepan of lightly salted water to the boil. Add the pasta, bring back to the boil and cook for 8–10 minutes, or until tender but still firm to the bite.

4 Meanwhile, stir the drained aubergines into the pan of tomatoes. Taste and adjust the seasoning, if necessary.

5 Drain the pasta and place in a warmed serving dish. Add the tomato and aubergine mixture, basil and half the pecorino cheese. Toss well, sprinkle with the remaining pecorino cheese and serve immediately.

VEGETABLES & DAIRY

TAGLIATELLE WITH PESTO

Serves: 4   **Prep: 15–20 mins**   **Cook: 15 mins**

Ingredients

450 g/1 lb dried tagliatelle

sprigs of fresh basil,
to garnish

Pesto

2 garlic cloves

25 g/1 oz pine kernels

5 g/4 oz fresh basil leaves

125 ml/4 fl oz olive oil

55 g/2 oz freshly grated
Parmesan cheese

salt

Method

1 To make the pesto, put the garlic, pine kernels
and a pinch of salt into a food processor or
blender and process briefly. Add the basil leaves
and process to a paste. With the motor still
running, gradually add the oil. Scrape into a
bowl and beat in the Parmesan cheese. Season
to taste with salt.

2 Bring a large, heavy-based saucepan of lightly
salted water to the boil. Add the pasta, return
to the boil and cook for 8–10 minutes, or until
tender but still firm to the bite. Drain well, return to
the saucepan and toss with half the pesto, then
divide between warmed serving dishes and top
with the remaining pesto. Garnish with sprigs of
basil and serve immediately.

VEGETABLES & DAIRY

PENNE WITH TWO CHEESES & WALNUTS

Serves: 4   **Prep: 15 mins**   **Cook: 15 mins**

Ingredients

350 g/12 oz dried penne

280 g/10 oz fresh or frozen peas

150 g/5½ oz soft cheese with garlic and herbs

175 g/6 oz baby spinach leaves

100 g/3½ oz blue cheese, cut into small cubes

115 g/4 oz walnuts, roughly chopped

salt and pepper

Method

1 Cook the pasta in a large saucepan of lightly salted boiling water for 8–10 minutes, adding the peas for the final 2 minutes. Drain, reserving 125 ml/4 fl oz of the hot cooking liquid.

2 Return the pan to the heat. Add the reserved cooking liquid and the soft cheese. Heat, stirring, until melted and smooth.

3 Remove from the heat, then add the spinach to the pan followed by the pasta, peas, blue cheese and walnuts. Season to taste with pepper and toss together, until the spinach has wilted and the cheese has started to melt. Serve immediately.

PENNE WITH ASPARAGUS & BLUE CHEESE

Serves: 4   **Prep: 15 mins**   **Cook: 25 mins**

Ingredients

450 g/1 lb asparagus spears

1 tbsp olive oil

225 g/8 oz blue cheese, crumbled

175 ml/6 fl oz double cream

350 g/12 oz dried penne

salt and pepper

Method

1 Preheat the oven to 230°C/450°F/Gas Mark 8. Place the asparagus spears in a single layer in a shallow ovenproof dish. Sprinkle with the oil and season to taste with salt and pepper. Turn to coat in the oil and seasoning. Roast in the preheated oven for 10–12 minutes until slightly browned and just tender. Set aside and keep warm.

2 Combine the cheese with the cream in a bowl. Season to taste with salt and pepper.

3 Bring a large saucepan of lightly salted water to the boil. Add the pasta, bring back to the boil and cook for 8–10 minutes, until tender but still firm to the bite. Drain and transfer to a warmed serving dish. Immediately add the asparagus and the cheese mixture. Toss well until the cheese has melted and the pasta is coated with the sauce. Serve immediately.

LINGUINE WITH LEMON, CHILLI & SPINACH

Serves: 4   **Prep: 15 mins**   **Cook: 25–30 mins**

Ingredients

350 g/12 oz dried linguine

2 tbsp olive oil, plus extra for drizzling

· 2 garlic cloves, finely chopped

1 red chilli, deseeded (optional) and finely chopped

finely grated rind and juice of 1 lemon

225 g/8 oz ricotta cheese

280 g/10 oz baby spinach, coarse stalks removed

4 tbsp freshly grated Parmesan cheese

salt and pepper

Method

1 Bring a large saucepan of lightly salted water to the boil. Add the pasta, bring back to the boil and cook for 8–10 minutes, until tender but still firm to the bite. Drain, reserving 6 tablespoons of the cooking liquid, then return to the pan. Drizzle with a little oil, toss gently and set aside.

2 Heat the oil in another saucepan, add the garlic and chilli and cook over a low heat, stirring frequently, for 2 minutes. Stir in the lemon rind and juice, ricotta cheese and reserved cooking liquid. Season to taste with salt and pepper and bring to simmering point, stirring frequently.

3 Add the spinach, in two to three batches, and cook for 2–3 minutes until wilted. Taste and adjust the seasoning, if necessary, then tip the sauce into the pan of pasta. Toss well, then divide between warmed plates. Sprinkle with the Parmesan cheese and serve immediately.

FUSILLI WITH COURGETTES & LEMON

Serves: 4   **Prep: 15 mins**   **Cook: 35–40 mins**

Ingredients

6 tbsp olive oil

1 small onion, very thinly sliced

2 garlic cloves, very finely chopped

2 tbsp chopped fresh rosemary

1 tbsp chopped fresh flat-leaf parsley

450 g/1 lb small courgettes, cut into 4-cm/1½-inch strips

finely grated rind of 1 lemon

450 g/1 lb dried fusilli

salt and pepper

4 tbsp grated Parmesan cheese, to serve

Method

1 Heat the oil in a large frying pan over a low–medium heat. Add the onion and cook gently, stirring occasionally, for about 10 minutes, until golden.

2 Increase the heat to medium–high. Add the garlic, rosemary and parsley. Cook for a few seconds, stirring.

3 Add the courgettes and lemon rind. Cook for 5–7 minutes, stirring occasionally, until just tender. Season to taste with salt and pepper. Remove from the heat.

4 Bring a large saucepan of lightly salted water to the boil. Add the pasta, bring back to the boil and cook for 8–10 minutes, until tender but still firm to the bite.

5 Drain the pasta and transfer to a warmed serving dish. Briefly reheat the courgette sauce. Pour over the pasta and toss well to mix. Serve immediately with the Parmesan cheese.

FETTUCCINE WITH PEPPERS & OLIVES

Serves: 4   **Prep: 15 mins**   **Cook: 45 mins**

Ingredients

100 ml/3½ fl oz olive oil

1 onion, finely chopped

200 g/7 oz black olives, stoned and roughly chopped

400 g/14 oz canned chopped tomatoes

2 red, yellow or orange peppers, deseeded and cut into thin strips

350 g/12 oz dried fettuccine

salt and pepper

freshly grated pecorino cheese, to serve

Method

1 Heat the oil in a large, heavy-based saucepan. Add the onion and cook over a low heat, stirring occasionally, for 5 minutes, or until softened. Add the olives, tomatoes and peppers and season to taste with salt and pepper. Cover and simmer gently over a very low heat, stirring occasionally, for 35 minutes.

2 Meanwhile, bring a large, heavy-based saucepan of lightly salted water to the boil. Add the pasta, return to the boil and cook for 8–10 minutes, or until tender but still firm to the bite. Drain the pasta and transfer to a warmed serving dish.

3 Spoon the sauce onto the pasta and toss well. Sprinkle generously with the pecorino cheese and serve immediately.

VEGETABLES & DAIRY

VERMICELLI WITH VEGETABLE RIBBONS

Serves: 20–25   **Prep: 20 mins**   **Cook: 20 mins**

Ingredients

350 g/12 oz dried vermicelli

3 courgettes

3 carrots

25 g/1 oz unsalted butter

1 tbsp olive oil

2 garlic cloves, finely chopped

85 g/3 oz fresh basil, shredded

25 g/1 oz fresh chives, finely snipped

25 g/1 oz fresh flat-leaf parsley, finely chopped

1 small head radicchio, leaves shredded

salt and pepper

Method

1 Bring a large, heavy-based saucepan of lightly salted water to the boil. Add the pasta, return to the boil and cook for 8–10 minutes, or until tender but still firm to the bite.

2 Meanwhile, cut the courgettes and carrots into very thin strips with a swivel-blade vegetable peeler or a mandolin. Melt the butter with the olive oil in a heavy-based frying pan. Add the carrot strips and garlic and cook over a low heat, stirring occasionally, for 5 minutes. Add the courgette strips and all the herbs and season to taste with salt and pepper.

3 Drain the pasta and add it to the frying pan. Toss well to mix and cook, stirring occasionally, for 5 minutes. Transfer to a warmed serving dish, add the radicchio, toss well and serve immediately.

VEGETABLES & DAIRY

CREAMY PAPPARDELLE & BROCCOLI

Serves: 4 **Prep: 15 mins** **Cook: 20 mins**

Ingredients

55 g/2 oz butter

1 large onion, finely chopped

450 g/1 lb broccoli, broken into florets

450 g/1 lb dried pappardelle

150 ml/5 fl oz vegetable stock

1 tbsp plain flour

150 ml/5 fl oz single cream

55 g/2 oz freshly grated mozzarella cheese

freshly grated nutmeg

salt and white pepper

fresh apple slices, to garnish

Method

1 Melt half the butter in a large pan over a medium heat. Add the onion and fry for 4 minutes.

2 Add the broccoli and pasta to the pan and cook, stirring constantly, for 2 minutes. Add the stock, bring back to the boil and simmer for a further 8–10 minutes. Season well with salt and white pepper.

3 Meanwhile, melt the remaining butter in a pan over a medium heat. Sprinkle over the flour and cook, stirring constantly, for 2 minutes. Gradually stir in the cream and bring to simmering point, but do not boil. Add the mozzarella cheese and season to taste with salt and a little freshly grated nutmeg.

4 Drain the pasta and broccoli mixture and return to the pan. Pour over the cheese sauce. Cook, stirring occasionally, for 2 minutes. Transfer the pasta and broccoli mixture to warmed serving dishes and garnish with a few slices of fresh apple. Serve immediately.

VEGETABLES & DAIRY

WILD MUSHROOM FUSILLI

Serves: 4   **Prep: 20 mins**   **Cook: 25–30 mins**

Ingredients

400 g/14 oz dried fusilli

60 g/2¼ oz hazelnuts

4 tbsp olive oil

1 onion, chopped

4 garlic cloves, chopped

300 g/10½ oz mixed
wild mushrooms (such as
oyster or chestnut),
roughly chopped

tbsp finely chopped fresh
flat-leaf parsley

salt and pepper

Method

1 Bring a large saucepan of lightly salted water to the boil. Add the fusilli, bring back to the boil and cook for 10–12 minutes, or until tender but still firm to the bite.

2 Dry roast the hazelnuts in a small, heavy-based frying pan for 3–4 minutes, or until the skins begin to brown. Turn them out of the pan onto a damp, clean tea towel, fold the tea towel over the nuts and roll them on the work surface to remove most of the skins. Chop the nuts roughly.

3 Heat the oil in a large saucepan over a medium heat. Fry the onion, garlic and mushrooms for 5 minutes, or until beginning to brown. Stir in the chopped nuts and continue to cook for another minute. Season to taste with salt and pepper.

4 Drain the pasta and toss together with the mushroom mixture and the fresh parsley to mix thoroughly. Serve immediately.

VEGETABLES & DAIRY

KALE, LEMON & CHIVE LINGUINE

Serves: 2–3   **Prep: 15–20 mins**   **Cook: 20 mins**

Ingredients

250 g/9 oz kale, tough stems removed, leaves sliced crossways into thin ribbons

225 g/8 oz dried linguine

8 tbsp olive oil

1 onion, chopped

1 garlic clove, very thinly sliced

grated rind of 1 large lemon

large pinch of dried red chilli flakes

3 tbsp snipped fresh chives

4 tbsp freshly grated Parmesan cheese

salt and pepper

Method

1 Bring a large saucepan of water to the boil. Add the kale and blanch for 2 minutes until just wilted. Drain, reserving the water, and set aside.

2 Return the reserved water to the pan and bring to the boil. Add the linguine and cook for 10–12 minutes until tender but still firm to the bite.

3 Meanwhile, heat the oil in a deep frying pan over a medium–high heat. Add the onion and fry for 2–3 minutes until translucent. Add the garlic and fry for a further minute.

4 Stir in the kale, lemon rind and chilli flakes and season to taste with salt and pepper. Cook over a medium heat for 4–5 minutes, stirring occasionally, until tender but still bright green. Add a little of the cooking water if the mixture becomes dry.

5 Drain the pasta and tip into a warmed serving dish. Add the kale, tossing with the pasta to mix. Stir in the chives, cheese, and salt and pepper to taste. Toss again and serve immediately.

KALE & ARTICHOKE GNOCCHI

Serves: 4

Prep: 30 mins, plus cooling

Cook: 1¼ hours– 1 hour 35 mins

Ingredients

200 g/7 oz shredded kale

2 tbsp olive oil

1 onion, chopped

400 g/14 oz canned artichoke hearts, quartered

2 garlic cloves, chopped

1 tsp red chilli flakes

juice of ½ lemon

2 tbsp pine nuts

salt

Gnocchi

675 g/1 lb 8 oz even-sized baking potatoes

250 g/9 oz plain flour, plus extra for dusting

2 tbsp olive oil

Method

1 To make the gnocchi, preheat the oven to 230°C/450°F/Gas Mark 8. Place the potatoes on a baking sheet and bake until fluffy all the way through – 45 minutes to an hour depending on the size of the potatoes. Leave to cool, then peel and mash the flesh with a potato ricer or masher until very smooth. There should be no 'bits'.

2 Turn the potato mash onto a floured board and knead, working in the flour and oil, for 5 minutes. Divide the mixture into four and roll each into a long snake. Use a knife to cut into pieces (around 2 cm/¾ inch long).

3 Bring a large saucepan of salted water to the boil. Add the kale, return to the boil and cook for 6–8 minutes. Drain and firmly press out any excess water.

4 Heat the oil in a frying pan over a high heat. Add the onion and fry for 3 minutes, then stir in the artichokes, garlic and chilli. Cook for a further minute, then stir in the kale, lemon juice and nuts.

5 Bring a large pan of salted water to the boil. Add a small batch of the gnocchi, return to the boil and cook for 2–3 minutes. Continue to cook batches of the remaining gnocchi in the same way. Mix thoroughly with the kale mixture and serve immediately.

VEGETABLES & DAIRY

FETTUCCINE ALL'ALFREDO

Serves: 4 **Prep: 15 mins** **Cook: 20-25 mins**

Ingredients

2 tbsp butter

200 ml/7 fl oz double cream

450 g/1 lb dried fettuccine

85 g/3 oz freshly grated
Parmesan cheese, plus
extra to serve

pinch of freshly
grated nutmeg

salt and pepper

1 fresh flat-leaf parsley sprig,
to garnish

Method

1 Put the butter and 150 ml/5 fl oz of the cream into a large pan and bring the mixture to the boil over a medium heat. Reduce the heat, then simmer gently for 1½ minutes, or until the cream has thickened slightly.

2 Meanwhile, bring a large pan of lightly salted water to the boil over a medium heat. Add the pasta and cook for 8–10 minutes, or until tender but still firm to the bite. Drain thoroughly and return to the pan, then pour over the cream sauce.

3 Toss the pasta in the sauce over a low heat, stirring with a wooden spoon, until coated thoroughly.

4 Add the remaining cream, Parmesan cheese and nutmeg to the pasta mixture and season to taste with salt and pepper. Toss the pasta in the mixture while heating through.

5 Transfer the pasta mixture to a warmed serving plate and garnish with the fresh parsley sprig. Serve immediately with extra grated Parmesan cheese.

RIGATONI WITH PEPPERS & GOAT'S CHEESE

Serves: 4　　　　**Prep: 15–20 mins**　　**Cook: 40 mins**

Ingredients

2 tbsp olive oil

1 tbsp butter

1 small onion,
finely chopped

4 red peppers, deseeded
and cut into
2-cm/¾-inch squares

3 garlic cloves, thinly sliced

450 g/1 lb dried rigatoni

125 g/4½ oz goat's
cheese, crumbled

15 fresh basil
leaves, shredded

10 black olives, stoned
and sliced

salt and pepper

Method

1 Heat the oil and butter in a large frying pan over a medium heat. Add the onion and cook until soft. Increase the heat to medium–high and add the peppers and garlic. Cook for 12–15 minutes, stirring, until the peppers are tender but not mushy. Season to taste with salt and pepper. Remove from the heat.

2 Bring a large saucepan of lightly salted water to the boil. Add the pasta, bring back to the boil and cook for 8–10 minutes, or until tender but still firm to the bite. Drain and transfer to a warmed serving dish. Add the goat's cheese and toss to mix.

3 Briefly reheat the sauce. Add the basil and olives. Pour over the pasta and toss well to mix. Serve immediately.

SPICY AUBERGINE, CHICKPEA & CORIANDER PENNE

Serves: 4   **Prep: 20 mins**   **Cook: 45–50 mins**

Ingredients

large pinch of saffron threads

450 ml/16 fl oz hot vegetable stock

2 tbsp olive oil

1 large onion, roughly chopped

1 tsp cumin seeds, crushed

350 g/12 oz aubergine, diced

1 large red pepper, deseeded and chopped

400 g/14 oz canned chopped tomatoes with garlic

1 tsp ground cinnamon

30 g/1 oz fresh coriander, leaves and stalks separated and roughly chopped

400 g/14 oz canned chickpeas, drained and rinsed

280 g/10 oz dried penne

salt and pepper

harissa or chilli sauce, to serve (optional)

Method

1 Toast the saffron threads in a dry frying pan set over a medium heat for 20–30 seconds, just until they begin to give off their aroma. Place in a small bowl and crumble with your fingers. Add 2 tablespoons of the hot stock and set aside to infuse.

2 Heat the oil in a large saucepan. Add the onion and fry for 5–6 minutes, until golden brown. Add the cumin seeds and fry for a further 20–30 seconds.

3 Stir in the aubergine, red pepper, tomatoes, cinnamon, coriander stalks, saffron liquid and remaining stock. Cover and simmer for 20 minutes.

4 Add the chickpeas to the pan and season to taste with salt and pepper. Simmer for a further 5 minutes, removing the lid to reduce and thicken the sauce if necessary.

5 Bring a large saucepan of lightly salted water to the boil. Add the pasta, bring back to the boil and cook for 8–10 minutes, until tender but still firm to the bite. Drain and transfer to a warmed serving bowl. Add the sauce and half the coriander leaves, then toss. Garnish with the remaining coriander and serve immediately with harissa, if desired.

VEGETABLES & DAIRY

FARFALLE WITH AUBERGINES

Serves: 4

Prep: 25 mins, plus draining & standing

Cook: 55 mins

Ingredients

1 large or 2 medium aubergines, diced

150 ml/5 fl oz olive oil

4 shallots, chopped

2 garlic cloves, finely chopped

400 g/14 oz canned chopped tomatoes

1 tsp caster sugar

350 g/12 oz dried farfalle

salt and pepper

fresh basil sprigs, to garnish

Method

1 Place the aubergine in a colander, sprinkling each layer with salt, and leave to drain for 30 minutes. Meanwhile, heat 1 tablespoon of the olive oil in a heavy-based saucepan. Add the shallots and garlic and cook over a low heat, stirring occasionally, for 5 minutes, or until softened. Add the tomatoes and their can juices, stir in the sugar and season to taste with salt and pepper. Cover and simmer gently, stirring occasionally, for 30 minutes, or until thickened.

2 Rinse the aubergine under cold running water, drain well and pat dry with kitchen paper. Heat half the remaining olive oil in a heavy-based frying pan, then add the aubergine in batches, and cook, stirring frequently, until golden brown all over. Remove and keep warm while you cook the remaining batches, adding the remaining oil as necessary.

3 Meanwhile, bring a large, heavy-based saucepan of lightly salted water to the boil. Add the pasta, return to the boil and cook for 8–10 minutes, or until tender but still firm to the bite. Drain the pasta and transfer to a serving dish.

4 Pour the tomato sauce over the pasta and toss well to mix. Top with the diced aubergine, garnish with fresh basil sprigs and serve.

VEGETABLES & DAIRY

PUMPKIN & TOMATO SPAGHETTI

Serves: 4   **Prep: 20 mins**   **Cook: 40–45 mins**

Ingredients

600 g/1 lb 5 oz pumpkin or
butternut squash, cut into
bite-sized pieces

2 red onions, cut
into wedges

1 tbsp olive oil

15 sun-dried tomatoes in oil

350 g/12 oz dried spaghetti

salt and pepper

fresh basil leaves, to garnish

Method

1 Preheat the oven to 180°C/350°F/Gas Mark 4.

2 Toss the pumpkin and onion together with the olive oil. Place in a roasting tin and roast in the preheated oven for 25–30 minutes, or until tender. Leave to cool for 5 minutes.

3 Cut the sun-dried tomatoes into small pieces and stir into the roasted vegetables. Season to taste with salt and pepper.

4 Bring a large saucepan of salted water to the boil. Add the spaghetti, return to the boil and cook for 8–10 minutes, or until tender but still firm to the bite.

5 Drain the spaghetti well and divide between four warmed serving plates. Top with the vegetables and garnish with fresh basil leaves. Serve immediately.

VEGETABLES & DAIRY

PASTA WITH GREEN VEGETABLES

Serves: 4   **Prep: 20 mins**   **Cook: 25–30 mins**

Ingredients

225 g/8 oz dried fusilli

head green broccoli, cut into florets

2 courgettes, sliced

225 g/8 oz asparagus spears, trimmed

125 g/4½ oz mangetout

125 g/4½ oz frozen peas

25 g/1 oz butter

3 tbsp vegetable stock

5 tbsp double cream

large pinch of freshly grated nutmeg

salt and pepper

2 tbsp chopped fresh flat-leaf parsley and 2 tbsp freshly grated Parmesan cheese, to serve

Method

1 Bring a large, heavy-based saucepan of lightly salted water to the boil. Add the pasta, return to the boil and cook for 8–10 minutes, or until tender but still firm to the bite. Drain the pasta in a colander, return to the saucepan, cover and keep warm.

2 Steam the broccoli, courgettes, asparagus spears and mangetout over a saucepan of boiling, salted water until just beginning to soften. Remove from the heat and plunge into cold water to prevent further cooking. Drain and reserve. Cook the peas in boiling, salted water for 3 minutes, then drain. Refresh in cold water and drain again.

3 Place the butter and vegetable stock in a saucepan over a medium heat. Add all the vegetables except for the asparagus spears and toss carefully with a wooden spoon to heat through, taking care not to break them up. Stir in the cream, allow the sauce to heat through and season to taste with salt, pepper and nutmeg.

4 Transfer the pasta to a warmed serving dish and stir in the chopped parsley. Spoon the sauce over and arrange the asparagus spears on top. Sprinkle with the freshly grated Parmesan and serve hot.

VEGETABLES & DAIRY

ZITI WITH ROCKET

Serves: 4

Prep: 20 mins, plus standing

Cook: 15–20 mins

Ingredients

2 fresh red chillies, thinly sliced, plus 4 whole chillies to garnish

350 g/12 oz dried ziti, broken into 4-cm/1½-inch lengths

5 tbsp extra virgin olive oil

2 garlic cloves, left whole

200 g/7 oz rocket

Parmesan cheese, grated, to serve

Method

1 For the red chilli garnish, use a sharp knife to remove the tip and cut the chilli lengthways, almost to the stem. Deseed and repeat the cutting process to create 'petals' of an equal length. Place the flowers in a bowl of iced water for 15–20 minutes to encourage the petals to fan out.

2 Bring a large saucepan of lightly salted water to the boil. Add the pasta, bring back to the boil and cook for 8–10 minutes, until tender but still firm to the bite.

3 Meanwhile, heat the oil in a large, heavy-based frying pan. Add the garlic, rocket and sliced chillies and fry for 5 minutes, or until the rocket has wilted.

4 Stir 2 tablespoons of the pasta cooking water into the rocket, then drain the pasta and add to the frying pan. Cook, stirring frequently, for 2 minutes, then transfer to a warmed serving dish. Remove and discard the garlic cloves and sliced chillies, garnish with red chilli flowers and serve immediately with the Parmesan cheese.

VEGETABLES & DAIRY

WHOLEWHEAT SPAGHETTI WITH EDAMAME BEANS

Serves: 4   **Prep: 10–15 mins**   **Cook: 15–17 mins**

Ingredients

350 g/12 oz dried wholewheat spaghetti

200 g/7 oz frozen edamame (soya) beans

2 tbsp extra virgin olive oil

2 garlic cloves, thinly sliced

finely grated rind of 1 lemon

salt and pepper

Method

1 Bring a saucepan of lightly salted water to the boil over a high heat. Add the spaghetti, return to the boil and cook for 10–12 minutes, or until tender but still firm to the bite. Add the edamame beans to the pan for the final 3 minutes. Drain the spaghetti and beans well and keep warm in the pan.

2 Meanwhile, place the oil in a small frying pan over a low heat and stir in the garlic. Reduce to a very low heat to infuse for about 10 minutes, stirring occasionally, without allowing the garlic to sizzle or brown.

3 Add the lemon rind, garlic and oil to the spaghetti and beans and toss to combine evenly. Season to taste with salt and pepper and serve immediately.

SPAGHETTI WITH FRESH PEA PESTO & BROAD BEANS

Serves: 4

Prep: 25 mins, plus cooling

Cook: 30–35 mins

Ingredients

250 g/9 oz shelled broad beans

500 g/1 lb 2 oz dried spaghetti

Pea pesto

300 g/10½ oz fresh shelled peas

75 ml/2½ fl oz extra virgin olive oil

2 garlic cloves, crushed

100 g/3½ oz freshly grated Parmesan cheese, plus extra shavings, to serve

100 g/3½ oz blanched almonds, chopped

pinch of sugar

salt and pepper

Method

1 To make the pesto, bring a saucepan of water to the boil. Add the peas, bring back to the boil and cook for 2–3 minutes, until just tender. Drain and transfer to a blender or food processor.

2 Add the oil, garlic and cheese and process to a coarse paste. Add the almonds and process again. Add the sugar and season to taste with salt and pepper. Set aside.

3 Bring a saucepan of lightly salted water to the boil. Add the beans, bring back to the boil and cook until just tender. Drain and leave to cool. Peel off the dull skins.

4 Bring a separate saucepan of lightly salted water to the boil. Add the spaghetti, bring back to the boil and cook according to the packet instructions, until tender but still firm to the bite. Drain, stir in the broad beans and toss with the pesto.

5 Turn out into a serving bowl, add a coarse grinding of pepper and serve immediately with cheese shavings scattered over the top.

CONCHIGLIE WITH MARINATED ARTICHOKE

Serves: 4 **Prep: 15 mins** **Cook: 1 hour–1 hour 5 mins**

Ingredients

280 g/10 oz marinated artichoke hearts from a jar

3 tbsp olive oil

1 onion, finely chopped

3 garlic cloves, crushed

1 tsp dried oregano

½ tsp dried chilli flakes

400 g/14 oz canned chopped tomatoes

350 g/12 oz dried conchiglie

4 tsp freshly grated Parmesan cheese

3 tbsp chopped fresh flat-leaf parsley

salt and pepper

Method

1 Drain the artichoke hearts, reserving the marinade. Heat the oil in a large, deep frying pan over a medium heat. Add the onion and fry for 5 minutes until translucent. Add the garlic, oregano, chilli flakes and the reserved artichoke marinade. Cook for a further 5 minutes.

2 Stir in the tomatoes. Bring to the boil, then simmer over a medium–low heat for 30 minutes. Season to taste with salt and pepper.

3 Bring a large saucepan of lightly salted water to the boil. Add the pasta, bring back to the boil and cook for 8–10 minutes, until tender but still firm to the bite. Drain and transfer to a warmed serving dish.

4 Cut the artichokes into quarters and add to the sauce with the Parmesan cheese and parsley. Cook for a few minutes until heated through. Pour the sauce over the pasta, toss well to mix and serve immediately.

MACARONI CHEESE

Serves: 4   **Prep: 20 mins**   **Cook: 30–40 mins**

Ingredients

250 g/9 oz dried macaroni

55 g/2 oz butter, plus extra for cooking the pasta

600 ml/1 pint milk

½ tsp grated nutmeg

55 g/2 oz plain flour

200 g/7 oz mature Cheddar cheese, grated

55 g/2 oz Parmesan cheese, grated

200 g/7 oz baby spinach

salt and pepper

Method

1 Cook the macaroni according to the instruction on the packet. Remove from the heat, drain, ad a small knob of butter to keep it soft, return to the saucepan and cover to keep warm.

2 Put the milk and nutmeg into a saucepan over low heat and heat until warm, but don't boil. Pu the butter into a heavy-based saucepan over a low heat, melt the butter, add the flour and stir to make a roux. Cook gently for 2 minutes. Add the milk a little at a time, whisking it into the roux then cook for about 10–15 minutes to make a loose, custard-style sauce.

3 Add three quarters of the Cheddar cheese and Parmesan cheese and stir through until they have melted in, then add the spinach, season with salt and pepper and remove from the heat

4 Preheat the grill to high. Put the macaroni into a shallow heatproof dish, then pour the sauce ove Scatter the remaining cheese over the top and place the dish under the preheated grill. Grill until the cheese begins to brown, then serve.

★ **Variation**

Add slices of steamed cauliflower or broccoli with the spinach for a more nutritious snack or side dish.

VEGETABLES & DAIRY

MEAT

SPAGHETTI CARBONARA

Serves: 4   **Prep: 20 mins**   **Cook: 25 mins**

Ingredients

400 g/14 oz dried spaghetti

4 eggs

4 tbsp double cream

55 g/2 oz grated Parmesan cheese, plus extra to garnish

55 g/2 oz grated pecorino cheese

1 tbsp butter

150 g/5½ oz pancetta, finely diced

salt and pepper

Method

1 Bring a large saucepan of lightly salted water to the boil. Add the pasta, bring back to the boil and cook for 8–10 minutes, until tender but still firm to the bite.

2 Meanwhile, stir together the eggs, cream, Parmesan cheese and pecorino cheese in a bowl. Season to taste with salt and pepper.

3 Melt the butter in a large saucepan, add the pancetta, and fry over a medium heat for 8–10 minutes, until crispy. Drain the spaghetti and add it to the pan while still dripping wet. Pour the cheese sauce over it. Remove the pan from the heat. Toss the spaghetti in the sauce until the eggs begin to thicken but are still creamy.

4 Transfer to warmed plates and serve immediately, sprinkled with pepper and a little more Parmesan cheese.

★ Variation

Cook the pancetta with two peeled garlic cloves, then remove once the meat is crispy, for an exciting flavour twist.

LINGUINE WITH BACON & OLIVES

Serves: 4 **Prep: 15–20 mins** **Cook: 15 mins**

Ingredients

3 tbsp olive oil

2 onions, thinly sliced

2 garlic cloves, finely chopped

175 g/6 oz rindless lean bacon, diced

225 g/8 oz mushrooms, sliced

5 canned anchovy fillets, drained

6 black olives, stoned and halved

450 g/1 lb dried linguine

25 g/1 oz freshly grated Parmesan cheese

salt and pepper

Method

1 Heat the olive oil in a large frying pan. Add the onions, garlic and bacon and cook over a low heat, stirring occasionally, until the onions are softened. Stir in the mushrooms, anchovies and olives, then season to taste with salt, if necessary, and pepper. Simmer for 5 minutes.

2 Meanwhile, bring a large, heavy-based saucepan of lightly salted water to the boil. Add the pasta, return to the boil and cook for 8–10 minutes, or until tender but still firm to the bite.

3 Drain the pasta and transfer to a warmed serving dish. Spoon the sauce on top, toss lightly and sprinkle with the Parmesan cheese. Serve immediately.

MEAT

PASTA WITH BACON & TOMATOES

Serves: 4   **Prep: 25 mins**   **Cook: 30–40 mins**

Ingredients

900 g/2 lb small,
sweet tomatoes

6 rashers rindless
smoked bacon

55 g/2 oz butter

1 onion, chopped

1 garlic clove, crushed

4 fresh oregano sprigs,
finely chopped

450 g/1 lb dried orecchiette

salt and pepper

freshly grated pecorino
cheese, to serve

Method

1 Blanch the tomatoes in boiling water. Drain, peel and deseed the tomatoes, then roughly chop the flesh.

2 Using a sharp knife, chop the bacon into small dice. Melt the butter in a saucepan. Add the bacon and cook for 2–3 minutes until golden brown.

3 Add the onion and garlic and cook over a medium heat for 5–7 minutes, until just softened.

4 Add the tomatoes and oregano to the pan and season to taste with salt and pepper. Lower the heat and simmer for 10–12 minutes.

5 Bring a large saucepan of lightly salted water to the boil. Add the pasta, bring back to the boil and cook for 8–10 minutes, until tender but still firm to the bite. Drain the pasta and transfer to a warmed serving bowl. Spoon the bacon and tomato sauce over the pasta, toss to coat and serve immediately with the pecorino cheese.

SPICY PASTA AMATRICIANA

Serves: 4　　　**Prep: 15–20 mins**　　　**Cook: 35 mins**

Ingredients

2 tbsp olive oil

1 large onion, finely chopped

2 garlic cloves, finely chopped

175 g/6 oz pancetta or bacon, diced

1–2 red chillies, deseeded and chopped, or ½–1 tsp crushed dried chillies

3 tbsp dry white wine

800 g/1 lb 12 oz canned chopped tomatoes

450 g/1 lb dried bucatini or spaghetti

85 g/3 oz pecorino cheese, freshly grated

salt and pepper

Method

1 Heat the oil in a large saucepan, add the onion and garlic and cook over a low heat, stirring occasionally, for 5 minutes. Add the pancetta and chillies, increase the heat to medium and cook, stirring frequently, for 5–8 minutes, until the onion is lightly browned.

2 Pour in the wine, bring to the boil and boil rapidly for 2 minutes, then stir in the tomatoes and season to taste with salt and pepper. Bring back to the boil, then reduce the heat to low and simmer, stirring occasionally, for 15 minutes.

3 Meanwhile, bring a large saucepan of lightly salted water to the boil. Add the pasta, bring back to the boil and cook for 8–10 minutes, until tender but still firm to the bite.

4 Drain the pasta, tip into the pan with the sauce and toss to coat. Transfer to a warmed serving dish, sprinkle with half the cheese and serve immediately, with the remaining cheese on the side.

MEAT

TUROS CSUSZA

Serves: 6   **Prep: 15 mins**   **Cook: 20 mins**

Ingredients

450 g/1 lb dried pasta
spirals or elbow macaroni

4 smoked back
bacon rashers

450 ml/16 fl oz
soured cream

350 g/12 oz
cottage cheese

salt

shredded fresh flat-leaf
parsley, to garnish

Method

1 Preheat the oven to 180°C/350°F/Gas Mark 4
and preheat the grill. Bring a large saucepan of
lightly salted water to the boil, add the pasta,
bring back to the boil and cook for 8–10 minutes
until tender but still firm to the bite.

2 Meanwhile, cook the bacon under the
preheated grill for 3–4 minutes on each side,
until crisp. Remove from the heat and crumble.

3 Drain the pasta, tip it into an ovenproof dish and
stir in the soured cream. Sprinkle with the cottage
cheese, then with the crumbled bacon and
lightly season with salt. Bake in the preheated
oven for 5 minutes, then serve straight from
the dish, garnished with the parsley.

MEAT

FARFALLE WITH GORGONZOLA & HAM

Serves: 4 **Prep: 15–20 mins** **Cook: 20 mins**

Ingredients

225 ml/8 fl oz crème fraîche

225 g/8 oz chestnut mushrooms, quartered

400 g/14 oz dried farfalle

85 g/3 oz Gorgonzola cheese, crumbled

1 tbsp chopped fresh flat-leaf parsley, plus extra sprigs to garnish

175 g/6 oz cooked ham, diced

salt and pepper

Method

1 Pour the crème fraîche into a saucepan, add the mushrooms and season to taste with salt and pepper. Bring to just below the boil, then lower the heat and simmer very gently, stirring occasionally, for 8–10 minutes, until the cream has thickened.

2 Meanwhile, bring a large saucepan of lightly salted water to the boil. Add the pasta, bring back to the boil and cook for 8–10 minutes, until tender but still firm to the bite.

3 Remove the pan of mushrooms from the heat and stir in the Gorgonzola cheese until it has melted. Return the pan to a very low heat and stir in the chopped parsley and ham.

4 Drain the pasta and add it to the sauce. Toss lightly, then divide among individual warmed plates, garnish with the sprigs of parsley and serve.

MEAT

PENNE WITH HAM, TOMATO & CHILLI

Serves: 4   **Prep: 15–20 mins**   **Cook: 1 hour 5 mins–1¼ hours**

Ingredients

1 tbsp olive oil

2 tbsp butter

1 onion, finely chopped

150 g/5½ oz cooked ham, diced

2 garlic cloves, very finely chopped

1 fresh red chilli, seeded and finely chopped

800 g/1 lb 12 oz canned chopped tomatoes

450 g/1 lb dried penne

2 tbsp chopped fresh flat-leaf parsley

6 tbsp freshly grated Parmesan cheese

salt and pepper

Method

1 Put the olive oil and 1 tablespoon of the butter in a large saucepan over a medium–low heat. Add the onion and fry for 10 minutes until softened and golden brown. Add the ham and fry for a further 5 minutes until lightly browned. Stir in the garlic, chilli and tomatoes. Season to taste with salt and pepper. Bring to the boil, then simmer over a medium–low heat for 30–40 minutes, until thickened.

2 Bring a large saucepan of lightly salted water to the boil. Add the pasta, return to the boil and cook for 8–10 minutes, or until tender but still firm to the bite. Drain and transfer to a warmed serving dish.

3 Pour the sauce over the pasta. Add the parsley, Parmesan cheese and the remaining butter. Toss well to mix and serve immediately.

MEAT

SAFFRON LINGUINE

Serves: 4

Prep: 15 mins, plus standing

Cook: 20 mins

Ingredients

350 g/12 oz dried linguine

pinch of saffron threads

2 tbsp water

140 g/5 oz cooked ham, cut into strips

175 ml/6 fl oz double cream

55 g/2 oz freshly grated Parmesan cheese

2 egg yolks

salt and pepper

Method

1 Bring a large saucepan of lightly salted water to the boil. Add the pasta, bring back to the boil and cook for 8–10 minutes, until tender but still firm to the bite.

2 Meanwhile, place the saffron in a saucepan and add the water. Bring to the boil, then remove from the heat and leave to stand for 5 minutes.

3 Stir the ham, cream and cheese into the saffron and return the pan to the heat. Season to taste with salt and pepper and heat through gently, stirring constantly, until simmering. Remove from the heat and beat in the egg yolks. Drain the pasta and transfer to a warmed serving dish. Add the saffron sauce, toss well and serve immediately.

MEAT

TAGLIATELLE WITH PARMA HAM & PUMPKIN SAUCE

Serves: 20–25   **Prep: 25 mins**   **Cook: 25–30 mins**

Ingredients

250 g/9 oz dried green or white tagliatelle

1 tbsp olive oil

freshly grated Parmesan cheese, to serve

Sauce

500 g/1 lb 2 oz pumpkin or butternut squash, peeled

2 tbsp olive oil

1 onion, finely chopped

2 garlic cloves, crushed

4–6 tbsp chopped fresh parsley

pinch of freshly grated nutmeg

about 300 ml/10 fl oz chicken stock or vegetable stock

115 g/4 oz Parma ham, cut into small pieces

150 ml/5 fl oz double cream

salt and pepper

Method

1 To make the sauce, cut the pumpkin in half and scoop out the seeds with a spoon. Cut the pumpkin into 1-cm/½-inch dice.

2 Heat the olive oil in a large saucepan. Add the onion and garlic and cook over a low heat for 3 minutes, or until soft. Add half the chopped parsley and cook for 1 minute.

3 Add the pumpkin pieces and cook for 2–3 minutes. Add the nutmeg and season to taste with salt and pepper. Add half the stock to the pan, bring to the boil, cover and simmer for about 10 minutes, or until the pumpkin is tender. Add more stock, if necessary.

4 Add the Parma ham to the pan and cook, stirring, for a further 2 minutes.

5 Meanwhile, to cook the pasta, bring a large saucepan of lightly salted water to the boil. Add the tagliatelle and olive oil and cook for 12 minutes, or until tender but still firm to the bite. Drain the pasta and transfer to a warm serving dish. Stir the cream into the pumpkin and ham sauce and heat through well. Spoon the mixture over the pasta, garnish with the parsley and serv immediately with the Parmesan cheese.

MEAT

RARE BEEF PASTA SALAD

Serves: 4

Prep: 20 mins, plus cooling (optional)

Cook: 15–20 mins, plus resting

Ingredients

450 g/1 lb rump or sirloin steak in 1 piece

450 g/1 lb dried fusilli

4 tbsp olive oil

2 tbsp lime juice

2 tbsp Thai fish sauce

2 tsp clear honey

4 spring onions, sliced

1 cucumber, peeled and cut into 2.5-cm/1-inch chunks

3 tomatoes, cut into wedges

3 tsp finely chopped fresh mint

salt and pepper

Method

1 Season the steak to taste with salt and pepper, then grill or pan-fry for 4 minutes on each side. Leave to rest for 5 minutes, then, using a sharp knife, slice the steak thinly across the grain and reserve until required.

2 Meanwhile, bring a large saucepan of lightly salted water to the boil. Add the pasta, bring back to the boil and cook for 8–10 minutes, until tender but still firm to the bite. Drain thoroughly and toss in the oil.

3 Mix together the lime juice, fish sauce and honey in a small saucepan and cook over a medium heat for about 2 minutes.

4 Add the spring onions, cucumber, tomato wedges and mint to the pan, then add the steak and mix well. Season to taste with salt.

5 Transfer the pasta to a large warmed serving dish and top with the steak mixture. Serve just warm or leave to cool completely.

MEAT

SPAGHETTI BOLOGNESE

Serves: 4 **Prep: 15–20 mins** **Cook: 30–40 mins**

Ingredients

350 g/12 oz spaghetti

fresh Parmesan cheese shavings, to garnish (optional)

sprigs of thyme, to garnish

crusty bread, to serve

Bolognese sauce

2 tbsp olive oil

1 onion, finely chopped

2 garlic cloves, finely chopped

1 carrot, peeled and finely chopped

85 g/3 oz mushrooms, peeled and sliced or chopped (optional)

1 tsp dried oregano

½ tsp dried thyme

1 bay leaf

280 g/10 oz lean beef mince

300 ml/10 fl oz stock

300 ml/10 fl oz passata

salt and pepper

Method

1 To make the sauce, heat the oil in a heavy-based, non-stick saucepan. Add the onion and sauté, half covered, for 5 minutes, or until soft. Add the garlic, carrot and mushrooms, if using, and sauté for a further 3 minutes, stirring occasionally.

2 Add the herbs and mince to the pan and cook until the meat has browned, stirring regularly.

3 Add the stock and passata. Reduce the heat, season to taste with salt and pepper and cook over a medium–low heat, half covered, for 15–20 minutes, or until the sauce has reduced and thickened. Remove and discard the bay leaf.

4 Meanwhile, bring a large saucepan of lightly salted water to the boil. Add the pasta, bring back to the boil and cook for 8–10 minutes, until tender but still firm to the bite. Drain well and mix together the pasta and sauce until the pasta is well coated. Serve immediately with crusty bread and garnished with Parmesan cheese shavings and sprigs of thyme.

MEAT

CREAMY BOLOGNESE PASTA

Serves: 4   **Prep: 15 mins**   **Cook: 30 mins**

Ingredients

2 tbsp olive oil

1 onion, finely chopped

500 g/1 lb 2 oz fresh pork mince

100 ml/3½ fl oz dry white wine

1 celery stick, chopped

1 garlic clove, crushed

2 bay leaves

200 ml/7 fl oz passata

100 ml/3½ fl oz double cream

450 g/1 lb dried penne

Method

1 Heat the oil in a large saucepan over a high heat, add the onion and mince and fry, stirring, until lightly browned.

2 Stir in the wine, celery, garlic, bay leaves and passata and bring to the boil. Reduce the heat, cover and simmer for 15 minutes.

3 Remove and discard the bay leaves. Stir in the cream and heat until boiling.

4 Meanwhile, bring a large saucepan of lightly salted water to the boil. Add the pasta, bring back to the boil and cook for 8–10 minutes, until tender but still firm to the bite. Drain and combine with the sauce.

5 Transfer to warmed serving bowls and serve immediately.

MEAT

SPICY SAUSAGE SALAD

Serves: 4   **Prep: 15–20 mins**   **Cook: 25–30 mins**

Ingredients

125 g/4½ oz
dried conchiglie

2 tbsp olive oil

medium onion, chopped

2 garlic cloves, very
finely chopped

small yellow pepper, de-
seeded and cut
into matchsticks

175 g/6 oz spicy pork
sausage, such as chorizo,
Italian pepperoni or salami,
skinned and sliced

2 tbsp red wine

1 tbsp red wine vinegar

125 g/4½ oz mixed
salad leaves

salt

Method

1 Bring a large saucepan of lightly salted water to
the boil. Add the pasta, bring back to the boil
and cook for 8–10 minutes, until tender but still
firm to the bite. Drain thoroughly and reserve.

2 Heat the oil in a saucepan over a medium heat.
Add the onion and cook until translucent. Stir in
the garlic, yellow pepper and sausage and cook
for about 3–4 minutes, stirring once or twice.

3 Add the wine, vinegar and reserved pasta to the
pan, stir and bring the mixture just to the boil over
a medium heat.

4 Arrange the salad leaves on warmed serving
plates, spoon over the warm sausage and pasta
mixture and serve immediately.

MEAT

SPAGHETTI WITH MEATLOAF

Serves: 4　　　　**Prep: 15 mins**　　　　**Cook: 25 mins**

Ingredients

2 tbsp olive oil

1 onion, chopped

1 garlic clove, finely chopped

400 g/14 oz meatloaf

3 tbsp brandy

400 g/14 oz canned chopped tomatoes

450 g/1 lb dried spaghetti

150 g/5½ oz frozen mixed vegetables

1 tbsp chopped fresh flat-leaf parsley

salt and pepper

freshly grated Parmesan cheese, to serve

Method

1　Heat the oil in a saucepan, add the onion and garlic and cook over a low heat, stirring occasionally, for 5 minutes until soft.

2　Crumble the meatloaf into the pan and cook, stirring frequently, for a few minutes. Meanwhile, bring a large saucepan of lightly salted water to the boil.

3　Add the brandy to the pan with the meatloaf, increase the heat to medium and cook for 5 minutes. Stir in the tomatoes. Bring to the boil, reduce the heat and simmer, stirring occasionally, for 10 minutes.

4　Meanwhile, add the pasta to the pan of boiling water, bring back to the boil and cook for 5 minutes. Add the frozen vegetables, bring back to the boil and cook for a further 5 minutes, until the pasta is tender but still firm to the bite. Drain the pasta and vegetables, add to the pan with the sauce and toss to coat. Season to taste with salt and pepper, sprinkle with the parsley and serve immediately, handing the Parmesan cheese separately.

MEAT

TUSCAN VEAL BROTH

Serves: 4

Prep: 20–25 mins, plus soaking & cooling

Cook: 2¾ hours– 2 hours 55 mins

Ingredients

55 g/2 oz dried peas, soaked for 2 hours and drained

00 g/2 lb boned neck of veal, diced

litres/2 pints beef stock

600 ml/1 pint water

55 g/2 oz pearl barley, rinsed and drained

1 large carrot, diced

1 small turnip bout 175 g/6 oz), diced

large leek, thinly sliced

d onion, finely chopped

100 g/3½ oz tomatoes, eseeded and chopped

1 sprig of fresh basil

100 g/3½ oz dried vermicelli

salt and white pepper

Method

1 Put the peas, veal, stock and water into a large pan and bring to the boil over a low heat. Using a slotted spoon, skim off any foam that rises to the surface.

2 When all of the foam has been removed, add the pearl barley and a pinch of salt to the mixture. Simmer gently over a low heat for 25 minutes.

3 Add the carrot, turnip, leek, onion, tomatoes and basil to the pan, and season to taste with salt and pepper. Leave to simmer for about 2 hours, skimming the surface from time to time to remove any foam. Remove the pan from the heat and set aside for 2 hours.

4 Set the pan over a medium heat and bring to the boil. Add the vermicelli and cook for 4–5 minutes. Season to taste with salt and pepper, then remove and discard the basil. Ladle into warmed serving bowls and serve immediately.

MEAT

PASTA WITH BEEF ROLLS

Serves: 4   **Prep: 30 mins**   **Cook: 40–45 mins**

Ingredients

2 garlic cloves

4 x 150-g/5½-oz very thin slices of lean beef

8 celery leaves

55 g/2 oz freshly grated Parmesan cheese

2 tsp capers, rinsed

4 tbsp olive oil

55 g/2 oz pancetta, diced

1 kg/2 lb 4 oz ripe plum tomatoes, peeled and chopped

400 g/14 oz dried orecchiette pasta

salt and pepper

Method

1 Finely chop 1 garlic clove and peel the other. Spread out the slices of beef on a work surface and season with salt and pepper. Place two celery leaves in the centre of each and scatter over the chopped garlic. Sprinkle with ½ teaspoon of the cheese and divide the capers between the beef slices. Roll up each slice and secure with a cocktail stick.

2 Heat the oil with the remaining garlic in a saucepan. When it begins to colour, remove and discard the garlic. Add the pancetta to the pan and cook over a medium heat, stirring frequently, for 2–3 minutes. Reduce the heat to low, add the beef rolls and cook, turning occasionally, for 8–10 minutes, until evenly browned. Add the tomatoes, season to taste with salt and pepper and simmer, stirring occasionally, for 25–30 minutes.

3 Meanwhile, bring a large saucepan of lightly salted water to the boil. Add the pasta, bring back to the boil and cook for 8–10 minutes, until tender but still firm to the bite. Drain thoroughly.

4 Remove the beef rolls from the sauce and add the pasta. Toss together, then divide between four plates. Top each with a beef roll, sprinkle with the remaining cheese and serve immediately.

BEEF STROGANOFF

Serves: 4

Prep: 20 mins,
plus soaking

Cook: 30 mins

Ingredients

15 g/½ oz dried porcini

350 g/12 oz beef fillet

2 tbsp olive oil

115 g/4 oz shallots, sliced

175 g/6 oz
chestnut mushrooms

400 g/14 oz pappardelle

½ tsp Dijon mustard

5 tbsp double cream

salt and pepper

fresh chives, to garnish

Method

1 Place the dried porcini in a bowl and cover with hot water. Leave to soak for 20 minutes. Meanwhile, cut the beef against the grain into 5-mm/¼-inch thick slices, then into 1-cm/½-inch long strips, and reserve.

2 Drain the porcini, reserving the soaking liquid, and chop. Strain the soaking liquid through a fine-mesh sieve or coffee filter and reserve.

3 Heat half the oil in a large frying pan. Add the shallots and cook over a low heat, stirring occasionally, for 5 minutes, or until softened. Add the soaked porcini, reserved soaking water and whole chestnut mushrooms to the frying pan and cook, stirring frequently, for 10 minutes, or until almost all of the liquid has evaporated. Transfer the mixture to a plate.

4 Meanwhile, bring a large saucepan of lightly salted water to the boil. Add the pasta, bring back to the boil and cook for 8–10 minutes, until tender but still firm to the bite.

Heat the remaining oil in the frying pan, add the beef and cook, stirring frequently, for 4 minutes, or until browned all over. You may need to do this in batches. Return the mushroom mixture to the pan and season to taste with salt and pepper. Place the mustard and cream in a small bowl and stir to mix, then fold into the meat and mushroom mixture. Heat through gently, then serve immediately with the freshly cooked pasta, garnished with chives.

PASTA & PORK IN CREAM SAUCE

Serves: 4

Prep: 25–30 mins, plus cooling

Cook: 45 mins

Ingredients

450 g/1 lb pork fillet, thinly sliced

4 tbsp olive oil

225 g/8 oz button mushrooms, sliced

1 tbsp lemon juice

pinch of saffron threads

350 g/12 oz dried orecchiette

4 tbsp double cream

12 quail eggs

salt

Red wine sauce

1 tbsp olive oil

1 onion, chopped

1 tbsp tomato purée

200 ml/7 fl oz red wine

1 tsp finely chopped fresh oregano

Method

1 To make the red wine sauce, heat the oil in a small heavy-based saucepan, add the onion and cook until transparent. Stir in the tomato purée, red wine and oregano. Heat gently to reduce and set aside.

2 Pound the slices of pork between 2 sheets of clingfilm until wafer thin, then cut into strips. Heat the oil in a frying pan, add the pork and cook for 5 minutes. Add the mushrooms and cook for a further 2 minutes. Strain and pour over the red wine sauce. Reduce the heat and simmer for 20 minutes.

3 Meanwhile, bring a large saucepan of lightly salted water to the boil. Add the lemon juice, saffron and orecchiette, return to the boil and cook for 8–10 minutes, or until tender but still firm to the bite. Drain the pasta thoroughly, return to the saucepan and keep warm.

4 Stir the cream into the saucepan with the pork and heat for a few minutes.

5 Boil the quail eggs for 3 minutes, cool them in cold water, then remove the shells and halve them. Transfer the pasta to a large, warmed serving plate, top with the pork and the sauce and garnish with the eggs. Serve immediately.

MEAT

CHILLI PORK WITH TAGLIATELLE

Serves: 4 **Prep: 20 mins** **Cook: 15 mins**

Ingredients

450 g/1 lb dried tagliatelle

3 tbsp peanut oil

350 g/12 oz pork fillet, cut into thin strips

1 garlic clove, finely chopped

1 bunch of spring onions, sliced

2.5-cm/1-inch piece fresh ginger, grated

2 fresh Thai chillies, deseeded and finely chopped

1 red pepper, deseeded and cut into thin sticks

1 yellow pepper, deseeded and cut into thin sticks

3 courgettes, cut into thin sticks

2 tbsp finely chopped peanuts

1 tsp ground cinnamon

1 tbsp oyster sauce

55 g/2 oz creamed coconut, grated

salt and pepper

2 tbsp chopped fresh coriander, to garnish

Method

1 Bring a large saucepan of lightly salted water to boil over a medium heat. Add the pasta, return to the boil and cook for 8–10 minutes, or until tender but still firm to the bite.

2 Meanwhile, heat the peanut oil in a preheated wok or large, heavy-based frying pan. Add the pork and stir-fry for 5 minutes. Add the garlic, spring onions, ginger and Thai chillies and stir-fry for 2 minutes.

3 Add the red and yellow peppers and the courgettes and stir-fry for 1 minute. Add the peanuts, cinnamon, oyster sauce and creamed coconut and stir-fry for a further 1 minute. Season to taste with salt and pepper. Drain the pasta and transfer to a serving dish. Top with the chilli pork, sprinkle with the chopped coriander and serve.

MEAT

ITALIAN SAUSAGE & PASTA SOUP

Serves: 4 **Prep: 20 mins** **Cook: 50–55 mins**

Ingredients

2 tbsp olive oil

1 onion, chopped

1 carrot, chopped

1 celery stick, chopped

450 g/1 lb Italian sausages, skinned and crumbled

2 garlic cloves, finely chopped

2 bay leaves

½ tsp dried oregano

1 tsp crushed chillies (optional)

400 g/14 oz canned chopped tomatoes

850 ml/1½ pints chicken stock

400 g/14 oz canned cannellini beans, drained

115 g/4 oz dried soup pasta, such as conchiglie

2 tbsp chopped fresh flat-leaf parsley

salt and pepper

freshly grated Parmesan cheese, to serve

crusty bread, to serve

Method

1 Heat the oil in a large saucepan, add the onion carrot and celery and cook over a low heat, stirring occasionally, for 5 minutes. Stir in the crumbled sausages and garlic, increase the heat to medium and cook, stirring frequently, for a further few minutes until the meat is brown.

2 Add the bay leaves, oregano, crushed chillies, if using, tomatoes and stock and bring to the boil, stirring frequently. Reduce the heat, partially cover and simmer for 30 minutes.

3 Stir in the beans and pasta and simmer for a further 5–8 minutes, until the pasta is tender but still firm to the bite. Season to taste with salt and pepper, stir in the parsley and remove from the heat. Remove and discard the bay leaves, ladle the soup into warmed mugs or bowls and serve immediately, with the cheese and crusty bread.

MEAT

SAUSAGE, BEAN & ROAST SQUASH CONCHIGLIE

Serves: 4   **Prep: 25 mins**   **Cook: 55 mins- 1 hour 5 mins**

Ingredients

1.25 kg/2 lb 12 oz butternut squash, peeled, deseeded and cut into 2.5-cm/1-inch chunks

3 tbsp olive oil

1 onion, finely chopped

1 celery stick, finely chopped

225 g/8 oz pork sausages with herbs, skins removed

200 ml/7 fl oz red wine

250 ml/9 fl oz vegetable or chicken stock

3 tbsp sun-dried tomato paste

400 g/14 oz canned borlotti beans, drained and rinsed

280 g/10 oz dried conchiglie

4 tbsp chopped fresh flat-leaf parsley

salt and pepper

freshly grated pecorino cheese, to serve

Method

1 Preheat the oven to 200°C/400°F/Gas Mark 6. Place the squash in a roasting tin, large enough to fit the squash in a single layer. Drizzle over 2 tablespoons of the olive oil. Toss together and roast for 25–30 minutes until tender.

2 Heat the remaining oil in a large frying pan. Add the onion and celery. Fry gently for 2 minutes until the onion turns translucent. Turn up the heat and add the sausage. Fry for another 2–3 minutes until lightly browned, breaking the sausage into small pieces as you stir.

3 Add the wine to the pan and boil rapidly until most of it has evaporated. Add the stock, sun-dried tomato paste and beans. Simmer for 10–12 minutes until the liquid has reduced and is slightly thickened.

4 Bring a large saucepan of lightly salted water to the boil. Add the pasta, bring back to the boil and cook for 8–10 minutes, until tender but still firm to the bite. Drain thoroughly and transfer to a warmed serving bowl. Add the roast squash, sausage sauce and parsley, and season to taste with salt and pepper. Serve immediately with the pecorino cheese.

MEAT

MEATBALLS IN A CREAMY SAUCE

Serves: 6

Prep: 30–35 mins, plus soaking

Cook: 20 mins

Ingredients

40 g/1½ oz fresh breadcrumbs

175 ml/6 fl oz milk

1 small onion, chopped

1 garlic clove, chopped

350 g/12 oz fresh beef mince

225 g/8 oz fresh pork mince

115 g/4 oz fresh veal mince

55 g/2 oz mashed potato

55 g/2 oz freshly grated Parmesan cheese

½ tsp ground allspice

1 tbsp chopped fresh flat-leaf parsley, plus extra to garnish

1 tbsp chopped sage

1 egg

5 tbsp plain flour

400 g/14 oz dried spaghetti

2 tbsp olive oil

175 ml/6 fl oz single cream

salt and pepper

Method

1 Put the breadcrumbs into a small bowl, add the milk and leave to soak. Put the onion and garlic into a food processor and process to a purée. Scrape into a large bowl and add the beef, pork, veal, potato, cheese, allspice, parsley, sage and egg. Drain the breadcrumbs and add to the bowl. Season with salt and pepper and mix well.

2 Shape the mixture into balls about 2.5 cm/1 inch in diameter by rolling between the palms of your hands. Put 4 tablespoons of the flour in a shallow dish and roll the meatballs in it to coat.

3 Bring a large saucepan of lightly salted water to the boil. Add the pasta, bring back to the boil and cook for 8–10 minutes.

4 Meanwhile, heat the oil in a frying pan, add the meatballs and cook over a medium heat, shaking the pan occasionally, for 10 minutes, until evenly browned and cooked through. Remove with a slotted spoon and keep warm.

5 Stir the remaining flour into the cooking juices in the pan. Add the cream and whisk for 3–4 minutes, but do not allow to boil. Season to taste and remove from the heat.

6 Drain the pasta and divide between six plates, then top with the meatballs. Spoon the sauce over and serve immediately.

MEAT

MACARONI WITH SAUSAGE, PEPPERONCINI & OLIVES

Serves: 4　　　　**Prep: 20 mins**　　　　**Cook: 25 mins**

Ingredients

1 tbsp olive oil

1 large onion, finely chopped

2 garlic cloves, very finely chopped

450 g/1 lb pork sausage, peeled and chopped

3 canned pepperoncini, drained and sliced

400 g/14 oz canned chopped tomatoes

2 tsp dried oregano

125 ml/4 fl oz chicken stock or red wine

450 g/1 lb dried macaroni

12–15 stoned black olives, quartered

75 g/2¾ oz grated Cheddar cheese

salt and pepper

Method

1 Heat the oil in a large frying pan over a medium heat. Add the onion and cook for 5 minutes, until softened. Add the garlic and cook for a few seconds, until just beginning to colour. Add the sausage and cook until evenly browned.

2 Stir in the pepperoncini, tomatoes, oregano and stock. Season to taste with salt and pepper. Bring to the boil, then simmer over a medium heat for 10 minutes, stirring occasionally.

3 Meanwhile, bring a large saucepan of lightly salted water to the boil. Add the pasta, bring back to the boil and cook for 8–10 minutes, or until tender but still firm to the bite. Drain and transfer to a warmed serving dish.

4 Add the olives and half the cheese to the sauce, then stir until the cheese has melted.

5 Pour the sauce over the pasta. Toss well to mix. Sprinkle with the remaining cheese and serve immediately.

MEAT

BROAD BEAN, CHORIZO & PASTA SALAD

Serves: 4-6

Prep: 25 mins,
plus standing

Cook: 20-25 mins

Ingredients

25 g/8 oz pasta shapes,
such as farfalle or fusilli

ring onions, some green
included, sliced

250 g/9 oz shelled baby
broad beans (frozen
or fresh)

100 g/3½ oz chorizo,
thinly sliced

tbsp extra virgin olive oil

shallots, finely chopped

2 tbsp red wine vinegar

2 tbsp chopped fresh
thyme or marjoram

squeeze of lemon juice

¼ tsp dried chilli flakes

salt and pepper

Method

1 Bring a large saucepan of lightly salted water to
the boil over a medium heat. Add the pasta and
cook for 8-10 minutes, or until tender but still firm
to the bite. Drain and transfer to a serving dish.
Add the spring onions, tossing to mix.

2 Meanwhile, put the broad beans in a pan of
boiling water. Bring back to the boil and cook for
4 minutes if frozen, 3 minutes if fresh. Drain under
cold running water and pat dry with paper
towels. Peel away the outer skins if they are
tough. Mix with the pasta and spring onions.

3 Cut the chorizo slices into quarters. Heat a
large frying pan over medium-high heat. Fry
the chorizo in a single layer for 3-4 minutes until
beginning to blacken slightly. Add to the pasta
mixture and toss well.

4 Reduce the heat to medium-low and warm
the olive oil. Add the shallots and gently fry for
2 minutes until soft. Swirl in the vinegar and cook
for a few seconds more. Tip the contents of the
pan over the pasta mixture and toss to coat.

5 Stir in the herbs, lemon juice, chilli flakes and
season to taste with salt and pepper. Toss
thoroughly to mix, then leave to stand at room
temperature for 30 minutes. Toss again and serve
at room temperature.

MEAT

RIGATONI WITH CHORIZO & MUSHROOMS

Serves: 4   **Prep: 15–20 mins**   **Cook: 15 mins**

Ingredients

4 tbsp olive oil

1 red onion, chopped

1 garlic clove, chopped

1 celery stick, sliced

400 g/14 oz dried rigatoni

280 g/10 oz chorizo sausage, sliced

225 g/8 oz chestnut mushrooms, halved

1 tbsp chopped fresh coriander

1 tbsp lime juice

salt and pepper

Method

1 Heat the oil in a frying pan. Add the onion, garli and celery and cook over a low heat, stirring occasionally, for 5 minutes, until softened.

2 Meanwhile, bring a large saucepan of lightly salted water to the boil. Add the pasta, bring back to the boil and cook for 8–10 minutes, unt tender but still firm to the bite.

3 While the pasta is cooking, add the chorizo to the frying pan and cook, stirring occasionally, for 5 minutes, until evenly browned. Add the mushrooms and cook, stirring occasionally, for a further 5 minutes. Stir in the coriander and lime juice and season to taste with salt and pepper.

4 Drain the pasta and return it to the pan. Add th chorizo and mushroom mixture and toss. Divide between warmed plates and serve immediate

MEAT

PEPPERONI PASTA

Serves: 4　　　**Prep: 15–20 mins**　　　**Cook: 25–30 mins**

Ingredients

3 tbsp olive oil

1 onion, chopped

1 red pepper, deseeded and diced

1 orange pepper, deseeded and diced

800 g/1 lb 12 oz canned chopped tomatoes

1 tbsp sun-dried tomato paste

1 tsp paprika

225 g/8 oz pepperoni sausage, sliced

2 tbsp chopped fresh flat-leaf parsley, plus extra to garnish

450 g/1 lb dried penne

salt and pepper

Method

1 Heat 2 tablespoons of the oil in a large heavy-based frying pan. Add the onion and cook over a low heat, stirring occasionally, for 5 minutes, or until softened. Add the red pepper and orange pepper, chopped tomatoes, sun-dried tomato paste and paprika and bring to the boil.

2 Add the pepperoni and parsley and season to taste with salt and pepper. Stir well, bring to the boil, then reduce the heat and simmer for 10–15 minutes.

3 Meanwhile, bring a large saucepan of lightly salted water to the boil. Add the pasta, bring back to the boil and cook for 8–10 minutes, until tender but still firm to the bite. Drain well and transfer to a warmed serving dish. Add the remaining olive oil and toss. Add the sauce and toss again. Sprinkle with parsley and serve immediately.

MEAT

TAGLIATELLE WITH LAMB

Serves: 4   **Prep: 30 mins**   **Cook: 40–45 mins, plus standing & resting**

Ingredients

750 g/1 lb 10 oz boneless lean lamb in a single piece

6 garlic cloves, thinly sliced

6–8 fresh rosemary sprigs

125 ml/4 fl oz olive oil

400 g/14 oz dried tagliatelle

55 g/2 oz butter

175 g/6 oz button mushrooms

salt and pepper

fresh pecorino cheese shavings, to serve

Method

1 Using a sharp knife, cut small pockets all over the lamb, then insert a garlic slice and a few rosemary leaves in each one. Heat 2 tablespoons of the oil in a large heavy-based frying pan. Add the lamb and cook over a medium heat, turning occasionally, for 25–30 minutes, until tender and cooked to your liking.

2 Meanwhile, chop the remaining rosemary and place in a mortar. Add the remaining oil and pound with a pestle. Season to taste with salt and pepper and set aside.

3 Remove the lamb from the heat, cover with foil and leave to stand. Bring a large saucepan of lightly salted water to boil over a medium heat. Add the pasta, bring back to the boil and cook for 8–10 minutes, until tender but still firm to the bite.

4 Meanwhile, melt the butter in another pan. Add the mushrooms and cook over a medium–low heat, stirring occasionally, for 5–8 minutes, until tender.

Drain the pasta, return it to the pan and toss with half the rosemary oil. Uncover the lamb and cut it into slices. Divide the tagliatelle between individual warmed plates, season with pepper and top with the lamb and mushrooms. Drizzle with the remaining rosemary oil, sprinkle with the pecorino cheese and serve immediately.

LINGUINE WITH LAMB & YELLOW PEPPER SAUCE

Serves: 4   **Prep: 15–20 mins**   **Cook: 1 hour–
1 hour 5 mins**

Ingredients

4 tbsp olive oil

280 g/10 oz boneless
lamb, cubed

1 garlic clove,
finely chopped

1 bay leaf

125 ml/4 fl oz dry white wine

2 large yellow peppers,
deseeded and diced

4 tomatoes, peeled
and chopped

250 g/9 oz dried linguine

salt and pepper

Method

1 Heat half the olive oil in a large, heavy-based
frying pan. Add the lamb and cook over a
medium heat, stirring frequently, until browned
on all sides. Add the garlic and cook for a further
minute. Add the bay leaf, pour in the wine and
season to taste with salt and pepper. Bring to the
boil and cook for 5 minutes, or until reduced.

2 Stir in the remaining oil, peppers and tomatoes.
Reduce the heat, cover and simmer, stirring
occasionally, for 45 minutes.

3 Meanwhile, bring a large saucepan of lightly
salted water to the boil. Add the pasta, bring
back to the boil and cook for 8–10 minutes,
until tender but still firm to the bite. Drain and
transfer to a warmed serving dish. Remove and
discard the bay leaf from the lamb sauce and
spoon the sauce over the pasta and toss. Serve
immediately.

★ Variation

Try adding ½ tablespoon crushed thyme into
the pan with the peppers for a more aromatic
sauce.

MEAT

POULTRY

CHICKEN SOUP WITH ANGEL HAIR PASTA

Serves: 4   **Prep: 20–25 mins**   **Cook: 30–35 mins**

Ingredients

3 large eggs

3 tbsp water

2 tbsp fresh chopped flat-leaf parsley

1 x 175-g/6-oz skinless boneless chicken breast

2 tbsp olive oil, plus extra for brushing

1.5 litres/2¾ pints chicken stock

115 g/4 oz dried angel hair pasta

salt and pepper

Method

1 Preheat the grill. Lightly beat the eggs with the water and stir in the parsley. Season the chicken with salt and pepper and brush with oil. Grill for 4–5 minutes on each side, until cooked through and the juices run clear, then remove from the heat and cut into thin strips.

2 Heat the oil in a 20-cm/8-inch omelette pan, then add a quarter of the egg mixture, swirling the pan to spread it evenly. Cook over a medium–low heat until the underside is set, then flip over with a spatula and cook for a further few seconds. Slide the omelette out of the pan and reserve. Cook three more omelettes in the same way, then roll them up and cut into thin slices to make threads.

3 Pour the stock into a large saucepan and bring to the boil. Add the pasta and bring back to the boil and cook for 5 minutes until tender but still firm to the bite. Add the chicken, season to taste with salt and pepper and cook for a further 3 minutes. Stir in the sliced omelette, remove from the heat and serve immediately.

★ Variation

Try adding 100g/3½ oz canned sweetcorn or cooked, diced button mushrooms while heating the soup.

POULTRY

CHICKEN & CHICKPEA SOUP

Serves: 4   **Prep: 20 mins**   **Cook: 2½ hours**

Ingredients

2 tbsp butter

3 spring onions, chopped

2 garlic cloves, crushed

1 sprig fresh marjoram, finely chopped

350 g/12 oz skinless, boneless chicken breasts, diced

1.2 litres/2 pints chicken stock

350 g/12 oz canned chickpeas, drained and rinsed

1 bouquet garni

1 red pepper, deseeded and diced

1 green pepper, deseeded and diced

115 g/4 oz dried macaroni

salt and white pepper

croûtons, to garnish

Method

1 Melt the butter in a large pan over a medium heat. Add the spring onions, garlic, marjoram and chicken and cook, stirring frequently, for 5 minutes.

2 Add the chicken stock, chickpeas and bouquet garni. Season to taste with salt and white pepper. Bring the soup to the boil over a medium heat. Reduce the heat and simmer for about 2 hours.

3 Add the diced peppers and pasta to the pan, then simmer for a further 20 minutes. Ladle the soup into warmed serving bowls and garnish with croûtons. Serve immediately.

POULTRY

CHICKEN, BACON & AVOCADO SALAD

Serves: 2

Prep: 20 mins,
plus cooling

Cook: 15–18 mins

Ingredients

150 g/5½ oz dried farfalle

2 thick rashers smoked streaky bacon

200 g/7 oz cooked skinless, boneless chicken breasts, sliced

2 plum tomatoes, sliced

1 large avocado, halved, stoned and sliced

35 g/1¼ oz rocket

salt and pepper

Dressing

6 tbsp olive oil

3 tbsp lemon juice

1 tsp Dijon mustard

1–2 garlic cloves, crushed

salt and pepper

Method

1 Bring a large saucepan of lightly salted water to the boil. Add the pasta, bring back to the boil and cook for 8–10 minutes, until tender but still firm to the bite. Meanwhile place all the ingredients for the dressing in a screw-top jar, and season to taste with salt and pepper. Place the lid on tightly and shake well to combine.

2 Drain the pasta and transfer to a large bowl. Ad half the dressing, then toss together and leave t cool. Preheat the grill to high.

3 Grill the bacon for 2–3 minutes, turning until crispy. Transfer the bacon to a chopping board and slice into chunky pieces. Add the pieces to the bowl of pasta with the chicken, tomatoes, avocado and rocket. Pour the remaining dressing over the top and toss well. Serve immediately.

PASTA & CHICKEN MEDLEY

Serves: 2

Prep: 20–25 mins, plus cooling

Cook: 15 mins

Ingredients

125–150 g/4½–5½ oz dried fusilli

2 tbsp mayonnaise

2 tsp pesto

1 tbsp soured cream or natural fromage frais

175 g/6 oz cooked skinless, boneless chicken, cut into strips

1–2 celery sticks, sliced diagonally

125 g/4½ oz black grapes, halved and deseeded

1 large carrot, cut into strips

salt and pepper

celery leaves, to garnish

Dressing

1 tbsp white wine vinegar

3 tbsp extra virgin olive oil

salt and pepper

Method

1 To make the dressing, whisk all the ingredients together until smooth.

2 Bring a large saucepan of lightly salted water to the boil. Add the pasta, bring back to the boil and cook for 8–10 minutes, until tender but still firm to the bite. Drain thoroughly, rinse and drain again. Transfer to a bowl and mix in 1 tablespoon of the dressing while hot; set aside until cold.

3 Combine the mayonnaise, pesto and soured cream in a bowl, and season to taste.

4 Add the chicken, celery, grapes, carrot and the mayonnaise mixture to the pasta, and toss thoroughly. Check the seasoning, adding more salt and pepper if necessary.

5 Arrange the pasta mixture on two plates, garnish with the celery leaves and serve.

SPICY CHICKEN PASTA

Serves: 4–6

Prep: 25 mins, plus marinating

Cook: 40 mins

Ingredients

12 skinless boneless chicken thighs, cubed

1 tbsp groundnut oil

1 red pepper, deseeded and chopped

1 green pepper, deseeded and chopped

200 g/7 oz canned chopped tomatoes

450 g/1 lb dried spaghetti

salt

Marinade

2 tbsp finely chopped spring onions, plus extra to garnish

1–2 chillies, deseeded (optional) and chopped

2 garlic cloves, finely chopped

1 tsp ground cinnamon

1 tsp ground allspice

pinch of grated nutmeg

2 tsp soft light brown sugar

2 tbsp groundnut oil

1 tbsp lime juice

1 tbsp white wine vinegar

salt and pepper

Method

1 Put the chicken into a large, non-metallic dish. Mix all the marinade ingredients in a bowl, mashing everything together. Spoon the mixture over the chicken and rub it in with your fingers. Cover the dish with clingfilm and leave to marinate in the refrigerator for at least 2 hours, preferably overnight.

2 Heat the oil in a saucepan, add the red pepper and green pepper and cook over a medium–low heat, stirring occasionally, for 5 minutes. Add the chicken and any remaining marinade and cook, stirring frequently, for 5 minutes until cooked through. Add the tomatoes, reduce the heat, cover and simmer, stirring occasionally, for 30 minutes. Check occasionally that the mixture is not drying out – if it is, add a little water.

3 Halfway through the chicken cooking time, bring a large saucepan of lightly salted water to the boil. Add the pasta, bring back to the boil and cook for 8–10 minutes, until tender but still firm to the bite.

4 Drain the pasta, tip it into the pan with the chicken and toss lightly. Transfer to warmed plates, garnish with the spring onion and serve immediately.

POULTRY

CHICKEN PASTA SALAD WITH WALNUTS

Serves: 4–6

Prep: 25 mins,
plus standing

Cook: 15 mins

Ingredients

115 g/4 oz egg
pappardelle, broken
into 7.5-cm/
3-inch lengths

coarsely grated zest of
1 lemon

2 tbsp extra virgin olive oil

4 carrots

2 courgettes

125 g/4½ oz cooked
chicken, sliced into
thin strips

40 g/1½ oz walnut halves

5 tbsp snipped fresh chives

2 tsp white wine vinegar

3 tbsp walnut oil

salt and pepper

Method

1 Bring a large saucepan of lightly salted water
to the boil over a medium heat. Add the pasta
and cook for 8–10 minutes, or until tender but
still firm to the bite. Drain thoroughly and tip
into a serving bowl. Toss with the lemon zest,
1 tablespoon of the olive oil and season to
taste with salt and pepper.

2 Meanwhile, trim and peel the carrots. Slice
lengthways into thin strips, using a mandolin
or very sharp knife. Trim the courgettes and
remove a wide band of peel on opposite sides.
Slice lengthways into thin strips, so that there is
narrow strip of green peel on each side. Put the
carrots in a steamer basket set over boiling wa
Steam for 3 minutes, then add the courgettes.
Steam for 2 minutes more until only just tender.

3 Add the vegetables, chicken, walnuts and chiv
to the pasta, tossing gently to mix. Whisk the
vinegar with ½ teaspoon of salt and ¼ teaspoo
of pepper. Whisk in the walnut oil and the
remaining tablespoon of olive oil. Pour over the
salad and toss again carefully. Leave to stand
for 30 minutes to let the flavour develop. Serve
at room temperature.

POULTRY

FARFALLE WITH CHICKEN, BROCCOLI & PEPPERS

Serves: 4   Prep: 15–20 mins   Cook: 25–30 mins

Ingredients

4 tbsp olive oil

5 tbsp butter

3 garlic cloves, very finely chopped

g/1 lb skinless, boneless chicken breasts, diced

¼ tsp dried chilli flakes

450 g/1 lb small broccoli florets

0 g/10½ oz dried farfalle

5 g/6 oz bottled roasted red peppers, drained and diced

ml/9 fl oz chicken stock

salt and pepper

Method

1 Bring a large pan of lightly salted water to the boil. Meanwhile, heat the oil and butter in a large frying pan over a medium–low heat. Cook the garlic until just beginning to colour.

2 Add the diced chicken to the frying pan, raise the heat to medium and cook for 4–5 minutes, until the chicken is no longer pink. Add the chilli flakes and season to taste with salt and pepper. Remove from the heat.

3 Plunge the broccoli into the boiling water and cook for 2 minutes until tender-crisp. Remove with a slotted spoon and set aside. Bring the water back to the boil. Add the pasta and cook for 8–10 minutes, or until tender but still firm to the bite. Drain and add to the chicken mixture in the pan. Add the broccoli and roasted peppers. Pour in the stock. Simmer briskly over a medium–high heat, stirring frequently, until most of the liquid has been absorbed.

4 Transfer to warmed dishes and serve.

POULTRY

FETTUCCINE WITH CHICKEN & ONION CREAM SAUCE

Serves: 4   **Prep: 20 mins**   **Cook: 35 mins**

Ingredients

1 tbsp olive oil

2 tbsp butter

1 garlic clove, very finely chopped

4 skinless, boneless chicken breasts

1 onion, finely chopped

1 chicken stock cube, crumbled

125 ml/4 fl oz water

300 ml/10 fl oz double cream

175 ml/6 fl oz milk

6 spring onions, green part included, sliced diagonally

35 g/1¼ oz freshly grated Parmesan cheese

450 g/1 lb dried fettuccine

salt and pepper

chopped fresh flat-leaf parsley, to garnish

Method

1 Heat the oil and butter with the garlic in a large frying pan over a medium–low heat. Cook the garlic until just beginning to colour. Add the chicken and increase the heat to medium. Cook for 4–5 minutes on each side, until cooked through and the juices run clear. Season to taste with salt and pepper. Remove from the heat. Remove the chicken from the pan, leaving the oil in the pan. Slice the chicken diagonally into thin strips and set aside.

2 Reheat the oil in the pan. Add the onion and gently cook for 5 minutes until soft. Add the crumbled stock cube and the water. Bring to the boil, then simmer over a medium–low heat for 10 minutes. Stir in the cream, milk, spring onions and Parmesan cheese. Simmer until heated through and slightly thickened.

3 Meanwhile, bring a large saucepan of lightly salted water to the boil. Add the pasta, bring back to the boil and cook for 8–10 minutes, until tender but still firm to the bite. Drain and transfer to a warmed serving dish. Layer the chicken slices over the pasta. Pour over the sauce, garnish with parsley and serve immediately.

PASTA WITH TWO SAUCES

Serves: 4   **Prep: 20–25 mins**   **Cook: 50–55 mins**

Ingredients

Tomato sauce

2 tbsp olive oil

1 small onion, chopped

1 garlic clove, chopped

400 g/14 oz canned chopped tomatoes

2 tbsp chopped fresh parsley

1 tsp dried oregano

2 bay leaves

2 tbsp tomato purée

1 tsp sugar

Chicken sauce

55 g/2 oz unsalted butter

400 g/14 oz skinless, boneless chicken breasts, cut into thin slices

85 g/3 oz blanched almonds

300 ml/10 fl oz double cream

350 g/12 oz dried green tagliatelle

salt and pepper

Method

1 To make the tomato sauce, heat the oil in a pan over a medium heat. Add the onion and cook until translucent. Add the garlic and cook for 1 minute. Stir in the tomatoes, parsley, oregano, bay leaves, tomato purée and sugar. Season to taste with salt and pepper, bring to the boil and simmer, uncovered, for 15–20 minutes, until reduced by half. Remove the pan from the heat and discard the bay leaves.

2 To make the chicken sauce, melt the butter in a frying pan over a medium heat. Add the chicken and almonds and cook for 5–6 minutes, or until the chicken is cooked through.

3 Meanwhile, bring the cream to the boil in a small pan over a low heat and boil for about 10 minutes, until reduced by almost half. Pour the cream over the chicken and almonds, stir and season to taste with salt and pepper. Reserve and keep warm.

4 Bring a large pan of lightly salted water to the boil over a medium heat. Add the pasta and cook for about 8–10 minutes, until tender but still firm to the bite. Drain and transfer to a warmed serving dish. Spoon over the tomato sauce and arrange the chicken sauce on top. Serve immediately.

POULTRY

CHICKEN WITH CREAMY PENNE

Serves: 2 **Prep: 10–15 mins** **Cook: 15–17 mins**

Ingredients

200 g/7 oz dried penne

1 tbsp olive oil

2 skinless, boneless chicken breasts

4 tbsp dry white wine

115 g/4 oz frozen peas

5 tbsp double cream

salt

4–5 tbsp chopped fresh flat-leaf parsley, to garnish

Method

1 Bring a large saucepan of lightly salted water the boil. Add the pasta, bring back to the boil and cook for 8–10 minutes, until tender but still firm to the bite.

2 Meanwhile, heat the oil in a frying pan, add the chicken and cook over a medium heat for about 4 minutes on each side, until cooked through and the juices run clear.

3 Pour in the wine and cook over a high heat until it has almost evaporated.

4 Drain the pasta. Add the peas, cream and pa to the frying pan and stir well. Cover and simmer for 2 minutes. Garnish with chopped parsley a serve immediately.

★ Variation

For an extra-indulgent treat, scatter 100g smoked lardons into the pan, along with the chicken.

POULTRY

CAJUN CHICKEN PASTA

Serves: 6   **Prep: 25 mins**   **Cook: 35–40 mins**

Ingredients

150 g/5½ oz butter

6 skinless boneless chicken breasts

3 tbsp plain flour

450 ml/16 fl oz milk

225 ml/8 fl oz single cream

6 spring onions, chopped

450 g/1 lb dried pasta shapes, such as fusilli or farfalle

40 g/1½ oz Parmesan cheese, grated

diced tomatoes and stoned black olives, to garnish

Spice mix

1 tbsp sweet paprika

1½ tsp salt

1 tsp onion powder

1 tsp garlic powder

1 tsp dried thyme

1 tsp cayenne pepper

½ tsp pepper

½ tsp dried oregano

Method

1 Heat a cast-iron frying pan over a high heat until very hot. Add 85 g/3 oz of the butter and melt over a low heat. Mix all the spice mix ingredients together in a shallow dish. Brush the chicken with the melted butter, dip into the spice mix to coat, shaking off the excess, and add to the pan. Cook for 5–8 minutes on each side until speckled with black, then remove the pan from the heat.

2 Meanwhile, melt 40 g/1½ oz of the remaining butter in a saucepan. Stir in the flour and cook for 1 minute. Remove the pan from the heat and whisk in the milk and cream, then return to the heat and bring to the boil, whisking constantly. Remove the pan from the heat.

3 Cut the chicken into thin strips and stir into the cream sauce with the spring onions. Return the pan to a medium–low heat and simmer, stirring frequently, for 20 minutes until the chicken is cooked through.

4 Meanwhile, bring a large saucepan of lightly salted water to the boil. Add the pasta, bring back to the boil and cook for 8–10 minutes, until tender but still firm to the bite. Drain, return to the pan, add the remaining butter and the cheese and toss well, then tip into a serving dish. Spoon the Cajun chicken on top, garnish with diced tomatoes and olives and serve immediately.

CREAMY CHICKEN & MUSHROOM TAGLIATELLE

Serves: 4

Prep: 20–25 mins, plus soaking　　**Cook: 25–30 mins**

Ingredients

25 g/1 oz dried shiitake mushrooms

350 ml/12 fl oz hot water

1 tbsp olive oil

6 bacon rashers, chopped

3 boneless, skinless chicken breasts, sliced into strips

115 g/4 oz fresh shiitake mushrooms, sliced

1 small onion, finely chopped

1 tsp finely chopped fresh oregano or marjoram

250 ml/9 fl oz chicken stock

300 ml/10 fl oz whipping cream

450 g/1 lb dried tagliatelle

55 g/2 oz freshly grated Parmesan

Method

1 Put the dried mushrooms in a bowl with the hot water. Leave to soak for 30 minutes until softened. Remove, squeezing excess water back into the bowl. Strain the liquid in a fine-meshed sieve and reserve. Slice the soaked mushrooms, discarding the stems.

2 Heat the oil in a large frying pan over a medium heat. Add the bacon and chicken, then cook for about 3 minutes. Add the dried and fresh mushrooms, the onion and oregano. Cook for 5–7 minutes, until soft. Pour in the stock and the mushroom liquid. Bring to the boil, stirring. Simmer briskly for about 10 minutes, continuing to stir, until reduced. Add the cream and simmer for 5 minutes, stirring, until beginning to thicken. Remove the pan from the heat and set aside.

3 Meanwhile, bring a large saucepan of lightly salted water to the boil. Add the pasta, bring back to the boil and cook for 8–10 minutes, or until tender but still firm to the bite. Drain and transfer to a serving dish. Pour the sauce over the pasta. Add half the Parmesan and mix. Serve with the remaining Parmesan.

PAPPARDELLE WITH CHICKEN & PORCINI MUSHROOMS

Serves: 4

Prep: 20–25 mins, plus soaking

Cook: 1 hour 5 mins

Ingredients

40 g/1½ oz dried porcini mushrooms

175 ml/6 fl oz hot water

00 g/1 lb 12 oz canned chopped tomatoes

esh red chilli, deseeded and finely chopped

3 tbsp olive oil

350 g/12 oz skinless, neless chicken, cut into thin strips

2 garlic cloves, finely chopped

350 g/12 oz dried pappardelle

salt and pepper

2 tbsp chopped fresh -leaf parsley, to garnish

Method

1 Place the porcini in a small bowl, add the hot water and soak for 30 minutes. Meanwhile, place the tomatoes and their can juices in a heavy-based saucepan and break them up with a wooden spoon, then stir in the chilli. Bring to the boil, then reduce the heat and simmer, stirring occasionally, for 30 minutes, or until reduced.

2 Remove the mushrooms from their soaking liquid with a slotted spoon, reserving the liquid. Strain the liquid into the tomatoes through a sieve lined with muslin and simmer for a further 15 minutes.

3 Meanwhile, heat 2 tablespoons of the olive oil in a heavy-based frying pan. Add the chicken and cook, stirring frequently, for 3–4 minutes until cooked through. Stir in the mushrooms and garlic and cook for a further 5 minutes.

4 Bring a large saucepan of lightly salted water to the boil. Add the pasta, bring back to the boil and cook for 8–10 minutes, until tender but still firm to the bite. Drain well, then transfer to a warmed serving dish. Drizzle with the remaining olive oil and toss lightly. Stir the chicken mixture into the tomato sauce, season to taste with salt and pepper and spoon onto the pasta. Garnish with parsley and serve immediately.

POULTRY

PENNE WITH CHICKEN & FETA

Serves: 4   **Prep: 15 mins**   **Cook: 15 mins**

Ingredients

2 tbsp olive oil

450 g/1 lb skinless, boneless chicken breasts, cut into thin strips

6 spring onions, chopped

225 g/8 oz feta cheese, diced

4 tbsp snipped fresh chives

450 g/1 lb dried penne

salt and pepper

Method

1 Heat the oil in a heavy-based frying pan. Add the chicken and cook over a medium heat, stirring frequently, for 5–8 minutes, or until golden all over and cooked through. Add the spring onions and cook for 2 minutes. Stir the feta cheese into the frying pan with half the chives and season to taste with salt and pepper.

2 Meanwhile, bring a large, heavy-based saucepan of lightly salted water to the boil. Add the pasta, return to the boil and cook for 8–10 minutes, or until tender but still firm to the bite. Drain well, then transfer to a warmed serving dish.

3 Spoon the chicken mixture onto the pasta, toss lightly and serve immediately, garnished with the remaining chives.

POULTRY

ITALIAN CHICKEN SPIRALS

Serves: 4   **Prep: 25 mins**   **Cook: 20 mins**

Ingredients

4 skinless, boneless chicken breasts

g/1 oz fresh basil leaves

15 g/½ oz hazelnuts

1 garlic clove, crushed

250 g/9 oz dried wholewheat fusilli

2 sun-dried tomatoes or fresh tomatoes

1 tbsp lemon juice

1 tbsp olive oil

1 tbsp capers

55 g/2 oz black olives

salt and pepper

Method

1 Beat the chicken breasts with a rolling pin to flatten evenly.

2 Place the basil and hazelnuts in a food processor and process until finely chopped. Mix with the garlic and salt and pepper to taste.

3 Spread the basil mixture over the chicken breasts and roll up from one short end to enclose the filling. Wrap each chicken roll tightly in foil so that they hold their shape, then seal the ends well.

4 Bring a large, heavy-based saucepan of lightly salted water to the boil. Add the pasta, return to the boil and cook for 8–10 minutes, or until tender but still firm to the bite. Meanwhile, place the chicken parcels in a steamer or colander set over the pan, cover tightly, and steam for 10 minutes.

5 Using a sharp knife, dice the tomatoes. Drain the pasta and return to the pan with the lemon juice, oil, tomatoes, capers and olives. Heat through. Pierce the chicken with a skewer to make sure that the juices run clear and not pink. Slice the chicken, arrange over the pasta and serve.

POULTRY

SPAGHETTI WITH PARSLEY CHICKEN

Serves: 4   **Prep: 15–20 mins**   **Cook: 25 mins**

Ingredients

1 tbsp olive oil

thinly pared rind of 1 lemon, cut into julienne strips

1 tsp finely chopped fresh ginger

1 tsp sugar

225 ml/8 fl oz chicken stock

250 g/9 oz dried spaghetti

55 g/2 oz butter

225 g/8 oz skinless, boneless chicken breasts, diced

1 red onion, finely chopped

leaves from 2 bunches of fresh flat-leaf parsley

salt

Method

1 Heat the oil in a heavy-based saucepan. Add the lemon rind and cook over a low heat, stirring frequently, for 5 minutes. Stir in the ginger and sugar, season to taste with salt and cook, stirring constantly, for a further 2 minutes. Pour in the stock, bring to the boil, then cook for 5 minutes, or until the liquid has reduced by half.

2 Meanwhile, bring a large saucepan of lightly salted water to the boil. Add the pasta, bring back to the boil and cook for 8–10 minutes, until tender but still firm to the bite.

3 Melt half the butter in a frying pan. Add the chicken and onion and cook, stirring frequently, for 5 minutes, or until cooked through and the juices run clear. Stir in the lemon and ginger mixture and cook for 1 minute. Stir in the parsley leaves and cook, stirring constantly, for a further 3 minutes.

4 Drain the pasta and transfer to a warmed serving dish, then add the remaining butter and toss well. Add the chicken sauce, toss again and serve immediately.

PENNE WITH CHICKEN & ROCKET

Serves: 4　　　**Prep: 25 mins**　　　**Cook: 25 mins**

Ingredients

25 g/1 oz butter

2 carrots, cut into thin batons

1 small onion, finely chopped

225 g/8 oz skinless, boneless chicken breast, diced

225 g/8 oz mushrooms, quartered

125 ml/4 fl oz dry white wine

125 ml/4 fl oz chicken stock

2 garlic cloves, finely chopped

2 tbsp cornflour

4 tbsp water

2 tbsp single cream

125 ml/4 fl oz natural yogurt

2 tsp fresh thyme leaves

115 g/4 oz rocket

350 g/12 oz dried penne

salt and pepper

fresh thyme sprigs, to garnish

Method

1 Melt the butter in a heavy-based frying pan. Add the carrots and cook over a medium heat, stirring frequently, for 2 minutes. Add the onion, chicken, mushrooms, wine, chicken stock and garlic and season to taste with salt and pepper. Mix the cornflour and water together in a bowl until a smooth paste forms, then stir in the cream and yogurt. Stir the cornflour mixture into the frying pan with the thyme, cover and leave to simmer for 5 minutes. Place the rocket on top of the chicken, but do not stir in, cover and cook for 5 minutes, or until the chicken is tender.

2 Strain the cooking liquid into a clean saucepan, then transfer the chicken and vegetables to a dish and keep warm. Heat the cooking liquid, whisking occasionally, for 10 minutes, or until reduced and thickened.

3 Meanwhile, bring a large saucepan of lightly salted water to the boil. Add the pasta, return to the boil and cook for 8–10 minutes, or until tender but still firm to the bite. Return the chicken and vegetables to the thickened cooking liquid and stir to coat.

4 Drain the pasta well, transfer to a warmed serving dish and spoon the chicken and vegetable mixture on top. Garnish with thyme sprigs and serve immediately.

POULTRY

CHICKEN, PROSCIUTTO & SUN-DRIED TOMATO POLPETTINI

Serves: 4–6

Prep: 25 mins, plus chilling

Cook: 30–40 mins

Ingredients

500 g/1 lb 2 oz fresh chicken mince

50 g/1¾ oz prosciutto, roughly chopped

3 tbsp finely chopped fresh flat-leaf parsley

1 egg, beaten

85 g/3 oz fresh breadcrumbs

1 onion, finely chopped

50 g/1¾ oz sun-dried tomatoes, finely chopped

2–3 tbsp vegetable oil

350 g/12 oz egg tagliatelle

salt and pepper

400 g/14 oz ready-made tomato pasta sauce, cooked, to serve

Method

1 Put the mince, prosciutto, parsley, egg, breadcrumbs, onion, tomatoes, and salt and pepper to taste into a large bowl and mix with your fingertips to combine.

2 Shape the mixture into about 30 small balls, place on a baking tray and chill for 30 minutes.

3 Heat half the oil in a large, non-stick frying pan, add half the meatballs and cook for 15–20 minutes, turning regularly until the chicken is thoroughly cooked. Drain the meatballs on kitchen paper. Repeat with the remaining oil and meatballs.

4 10 minutes before the end of cooking time, bring a large saucepan of lightly salted water to the boil. Add the pasta, return to the boil and cook for 8-10 minutes, or until tender but still firm to the bite.

5 Drain the pasta and transfer to a warmed serving dish. Pour over the cooked tomato sauce and top with the meatballs. Serve immediately.

TURKEY PASTA PESTO

Serves: 4   **Prep: 15–20 mins**   **Cook: 17 mins**

Ingredients

150 g/5½ oz dried trofie pasta or thin penne pasta

100 g/3½ oz new potatoes, scrubbed and thinly sliced

100 g/3½ oz fine French beans, topped and tailed and cut about the same length as the pasta

2 tbsp olive oil

450 g/1 lb fresh turkey mince

2 large garlic cloves, crushed

150 g/5½ oz pesto

salt and pepper

freshly grated Parmesan cheese or pecorino cheese, to serve

Method

1 Bring a large saucepan of water to the boil with 1 teaspoon of salt. Add the pasta, bring back to the boil and cook for 12 minutes, until tender but still firm to the bite. Add the potatoes 7 minutes before the end of the cooking time, then add the beans 2 minutes later.

2 Meanwhile, heat the oil in a large frying pan over a medium–high heat. Add the turkey and fry, stirring with a wooden spoon to break it up into large clumps, for about 5 minutes until just starting to brown. Add the garlic and fry for a further minute, or until the turkey is cooked through. Remove from the pan and keep hot.

3 When the pasta and vegetables are tender, drain, reserving a few tablespoons of the cooking water. Return the pasta and vegetables to the pan, add the turkey and pesto and toss together well. Add a little of the reserved cooking water, if necessary. Season to taste with salt and pepper.

4 Divide the mixture between warmed bowls and serve immediately, with plenty of cheese for sprinkling over.

TURKEY PASTA PRIMAVERA

Serves: 4   **Prep: 15–20 mins**   **Cook: 25–35 mins**

Ingredients

25 g/1 oz butter

2 tbsp olive oil

2 shallots, finely chopped

1 garlic clove,
finely chopped

500 g/1 lb 2 oz diced turkey

115 g/4 oz asparagus tips

2 carrots, thinly
sliced diagonally

115 g/4 oz mushrooms,
thinly sliced

1 tbsp chopped fresh sage

1 tbsp chopped fresh
flat-leaf parsley

150 ml/5 fl oz dry white wine

175 ml/6 fl oz double cream

300 g/10½ oz dried pasta
shapes, such as farfalle

55 g/2 oz freshly grated
Parmesan cheese

salt and pepper

Method

1 Melt the butter with the oil in a large frying pa
add the shallots and garlic and cook over a
low heat, stirring occasionally, for 3–4 minutes
until soft. Add the turkey, increase the heat to
medium and cook, stirring frequently, for
6–8 minutes until cooked through.

2 Add the asparagus tips, carrots and mushroor
and cook, gently stirring occasionally, for
4–5 minutes until starting to soften, then add th
herbs, wine and cream. Reduce the heat and
simmer stirring occasionally, for 10–15 minutes
until the vegetables are tender.

3 Meanwhile, bring a large saucepan of lightly
salted water to the boil. Add the pasta, bring
back to the boil and cook for 8–10 minutes, un
tender but still firm to the bite. Drain the pasta
it into the pan of sauce, season to taste with s
and pepper and toss well. Transfer to a warme
serving dish, sprinkle with the cheese and
serve immediately.

PASTA WITH HARISSA TURKEY MEATBALLS

Serves: 4   **Prep: 25 mins**   **Cook: 20 mins**

Ingredients

350 g/12 oz fresh turkey mince

55 g/2 oz dry breadcrumbs

6 tbsp Greek-style yogurt

1 egg

½ tsp ground coriander

½ tsp ground cumin

½–1 tsp harissa

3 tbsp finely chopped parsley

350 g/12 oz dried spaghetti or tagliatelle

olive oil, for drizzling

salt and pepper

Sauce

400 g/14 oz canned chopped tomatoes

1 small chilli, deseeded and finely chopped

¼ tsp ground cinnamon

½ tsp ground cumin

Method

1 Preheat the oven to 200°C/400°F/Gas Mark 6. Line a baking sheet with baking paper.

2 Mix together the turkey, breadcrumbs, yogurt, egg, coriander, cumin, harissa and parsley in a bowl until thoroughly combined. Season to taste with salt and pepper. Shape the mixture into meatballs about the size of a golf ball and put them on the prepared baking sheet. Bake for 15 minutes until lightly browned.

3 Meanwhile, bring a large saucepan of lightly salted water to the boil. Add the pasta, bring back to the boil and cook for 8–10 minutes, until tender but still firm to the bite. Drain, transfer to a warmed dish, drizzle with oil and toss to coat.

4 Meanwhile, put all the sauce ingredients into a saucepan and simmer, stirring occasionally, for 5 minutes until thickened.

5 Remove the meatballs from the oven and add to the pasta. Pour the sauce over them and toss together. Serve immediately.

MEXICAN SPAGHETTI & MEATBALLS

Serves: 4 **Prep: 30 mins** **Cook: 45 mins**

Ingredients

1 tbsp olive oil, plus extra for greasing

450 g/1 lb fresh turkey mince

½–1 tsp dried crushed chillies

1 tbsp freshly grated Parmesan cheese

1 egg, lightly beaten

1 small onion, finely chopped

1–2 red chillies, deseeded (optional) and finely chopped

2 tostadas, crumbled

4 tbsp fresh breadcrumbs

350 g/12 oz dried spaghetti

salt

Sauce

1 tbsp olive oil

1 small onion, chopped

1 garlic clove, finely chopped

1 chipotle chilli, finely chopped

1 tbsp tequila (optional)

400 g/14 oz canned chopped tomatoes

1 tbsp taco spice seasoning

1 tbsp chopped fresh coriander

Method

1 Preheat the oven to 180°C/350°F/Gas Mark 4 and brush a baking sheet with oil. Mix together the turkey, dried chillies, cheese, egg, onion, fresh chillies, crumbled tostadas and breadcrumbs a bowl and season to taste with salt. When the mixture is combined, shape small pieces into balls, rolling them between your palms.

2 Put the balls on the prepared baking sheet an bake in the preheated oven for 20 minutes, the turn over and bake for a further 20 minutes.

3 Meanwhile, make the sauce. Heat the oil in a saucepan, add the onion, garlic and chilli and cook over a low heat, stirring occasionally, for 5 minutes. Add the tequila, if using, and cook for a further few minutes until the alcohol has evaporated, then add the tomatoes and stir in the spice seasoning. Simmer for 15 minutes.

4 Meanwhile, bring a large saucepan of lightly salted water to the boil. Add the pasta, bring back to the boil and cook for 8–10 minutes, un tender but still firm to the bite.

5 When the meatballs are cooked, remove from the oven, add to the sauce and stir in the coriander. Simmer for 5 minutes. Drain the past and tip it into a warmed serving dish. Add the meatballs and sauce and serve immediately.

POULTRY

TURKEY TAGLIATELLE WITH LEMON PEPPER CREAM SAUCE

Serves: 4 **Prep: 20–25 mins** **Cook: 30 mins**

Ingredients

450 g/1 lb turkey steaks

grated zest of 1 lemon

2 tsp cracked
black peppercorns

350 g/12 oz egg tagliatelle

1 tbsp olive oil

55 g/2 oz butter

juice of ½ lemon

250 ml/9 fl oz double cream

4 tbsp chopped
fresh flat-leaf parsley

salt

Method

1 Place the turkey steaks between two sheets of clingfilm and flatten with a mallet. Slice the meat across the grain into thin strips measuring 1 x 9 cm/½ x 3½ inches. Put the strips in a shallow dish and toss with the lemon zest and the pepper.

2 Meanwhile, bring a large saucepan of lightly salted water to the boil. Add the pasta, return the boil and cook for 8–10 minutes, or until tender but still firm to the bite.

3 Heat the oil and half the butter in a saucepan and fry the turkey strips for 5 minutes until no longer pink. Season to taste with salt, then transfer to a plate and keep warm.

4 Add the remaining butter to the pan. Stir in the lemon juice and simmer for a few seconds. Pour in the cream, bring to the boil, then reduce the heat and simmer for 5 minutes, stirring often. Return the turkey to the pan, stirring until well coated with the cream.

5 Drain the pasta, reserving 4 tablespoons of the cooking water. Tip the pasta into a warmed serving dish. Stir the cooking water into the turkey mixture, then add the parsley. Pour the sauce over the pasta, and toss to mix. Serve immediately.

POULTRY

CREAMY TURKEY & BROCCOLI GNOCCHI

rves: 4   **Prep: 15–20 mins**   **Cook: 10 mins**

Ingredients

1 tbsp sunflower oil

500 g/1 lb 2 oz turkey
stir-fry strips

2 small leeks,
sliced diagonally

1 lb 2 oz ready-made
fresh gnocchi

7 oz broccoli, cut into
bite-sized pieces

g/3 oz crème fraîche

wholegrain mustard

3 tbsp orange juice

3 tbsp pine kernels

salt and pepper

Method

1 Heat the oil in a wok or large frying pan, then add the turkey and leeks and stir-fry over a high heat for 5–6 minutes.

2 Meanwhile, bring a saucepan of lightly salted water to the boil. Add the gnocchi and broccoli, then cook for 3–4 minutes.

3 Drain the gnocchi and broccoli and stir into the turkey mixture.

4 Mix together the crème fraîche, mustard and orange juice in a small bowl. Season to taste with salt and pepper, then stir into the wok.

5 Transfer to a warmed serving dish, sprinkle with the pine kernels and serve immediately.

POULTRY

PASTA WITH CHILLI BARBECUE SAUCE

Serves: 4　　　　**Prep: 20–25 mins**　　　　**Cook: 30 mins**

Ingredients

2 tbsp olive oil

2 garlic cloves, finely chopped

1 large onion, finely chopped

2 red peppers, deseeded and chopped

1–2 chillies, deseeded (optional) and finely chopped

450 g/1 lb fresh turkey mince

325 g/11½ oz canned sweetcorn, drained

400 g/14 oz ready-made tomato pasta sauce

2 tbsp Worcestershire sauce

1 tbsp red wine vinegar

1 tbsp soft light brown sugar

350 g/12 oz dried fusilli

2 tbsp chopped fresh flat-leaf parsley

salt and pepper

pickled chillies, drained and sliced, to garnish (optional)

Method

1 Heat the oil in a frying pan, add the garlic, on red peppers and chillies and cook over a low heat, stirring occasionally, for 5 minutes. Increa the heat to medium, add the turkey and coo stirring frequently, for 5–8 minutes until cooked through.

2 Stir in the sweetcorn, tomato pasta sauce, Worcestershire sauce, vinegar and sugar. Sea to taste with salt and pepper and simmer for 15 minutes.

3 Meanwhile, bring a large saucepan of lightly salted water to the boil. Add the pasta, bring back to the boil and cook for 8–10 minutes, u tender but still firm to the bite. Drain and tip in the pan of sauce. Add the parsley, taste and adjust the seasoning, if necessary, and remove from the heat. Transfer to a warmed serving dish and serve immediately, garnished with th pickled chillies, if using.

GIANT PASTA SHELLS WITH TURKEY

Serves: 4　　　　**Prep: 25 mins**　　　　**Cook: 45 mins**

Ingredients

450 ml/16 fl oz passata

16 giant dried pasta shells

3 tbsp olive oil

1 onion, finely chopped

2 garlic cloves, finely chopped

450 g/1 lb fresh turkey mince

1 tbsp sun-dried tomato purée

1 tbsp finely chopped fresh flat-leaf parsley

225 g/8 oz mozzarella cheese, shredded

1–2 tsp black olive paste

salt and pepper

Method

1　Pour the passata into a nylon strainer set over bowl and set aside. Bring a large saucepan of lightly salted water to the boil. Add the pasta, bring back to the boil and cook for 8–10 minu until tender but still firm to the bite. Drain and set aside. Preheat the oven to 180°C/350°F/Ga Mark 4.

2　Meanwhile, heat 2 tablespoons of the oil in a frying pan, add the onion and half the garlic a cook over a low heat, stirring occasionally, for minutes until soft. Add the turkey, increase the heat to medium and cook, stirring occasional for 8–10 minutes until cooked through. Stir in th tomato purée, parsley and half the cheese, season to taste with salt and pepper and remove the pan from the heat.

3　Tip the passata from the strainer into a bowl a stir in the olive paste and the remaining oil and garlic. Spread half this mixture over the base of an ovenproof dish. Divide the turkey mixture between the pasta shells and put them in the dish, meat-side up, then pour the remaining passata mixture over them. Cover the dish with foil and bake in the preheated oven for 25 minutes.

Remove the dish from the oven and discard the foil. Sprinkle the remaining cheese over the pasta, return the dish to the oven and bake for a further 5 minutes, until the cheese has melted. Serve immediately.

CONCHIGLIE WITH BALSAMIC-GLAZED DUCK & MUSHROOMS

Serves: 3-4　　　**Prep: 30 mins**　　　**Cook: 1 hour 35 mins-1 hour 55 mins**

Ingredients

4 duck legs, halved

125 ml/4 fl oz good-quality balsamic vinegar

2 tbsp olive oil, for frying

1 onion, finely chopped

1 carrot, finely chopped

1 celery stick, finely chopped

1 large garlic clove, finely chopped

125 g/4½ oz chestnut mushrooms, thinly sliced

400 ml/14 fl oz chicken stock

1 tbsp tomato purée

½ tsp dried oregano

squeeze of lemon juice

4 tbsp chopped fresh flat-leaf parsley

350 g/12 oz conchiglie

salt and pepper

Method

1　Remove the skin from the duck legs and discard. Place the joints in a frying pan and pour in the vinegar, simmer and turn frequently for 10 minutes. Reduce the heat for 5 minutes then remove the pan from the heat. Heat the oil in a saucepan and add the onion, carrot, celery and garlic and gently fry over a medium heat until soft but not coloured. Stir in the mushrooms and cook for another 5 minutes then place the duck joints on top of the vegetables.

2　Pour the stock over the duck then stir in the purée and oregano. Bring to the boil, then reduce the heat and simmer for 45–60 minutes, stirring occasionally, until the duck is tender.

3　Remove the duck from the pan, using tongs. Simmer the sauce for a few minutes until slightly thickened and reduced. Strip the duck meat from the bones, chop it into small pieces and put back in the pan. Add a squeeze of lemon juice, the parsley and season to taste with salt and pepper. Simmer gently for 5 minutes.

4　Bring a large saucepan of lightly salted water to the boil. Add the pasta, return to the boil and cook for 8–10 minutes, or until tender but still firm to the bite. Drain and transfer to a warmed serving dish. Toss with the sauce and serve immediately.

FETTUCCINE WITH DUCK SAUCE

Serves: 4 **Prep: 30–35 mins** **Cook: 1¾ hours– 1 hour 50 mins**

Ingredients

4 tbsp olive oil

4 duck legs

1 shallot, finely chopped

1 leek, white part only, finely chopped

1 garlic clove, finely chopped

1 celery stick, finely chopped

1 carrot, finely chopped

4 pancetta or bacon slices, diced

1 tbsp finely chopped fresh flat-leaf parsley

1 bay leaf

5 tbsp dry white wine

400 g/14 oz canned chopped tomatoes

2 tbsp tomato purée

pinch of sugar

450 g/1 lb dried fettuccine

salt and pepper

freshly grated Parmesan cheese, to serve

Method

1 Heat half the oil in a frying pan. Add the duck and cook over a medium heat, turning frequently, for 8–10 minutes, until golden brown. Using a slotted spoon, transfer to a large saucepan.

2 Wipe out the frying pan with kitchen paper, then add the remaining oil. Add the shallot, leek, garlic, celery, carrot and pancetta and cook over a low heat, stirring, for 10 minutes. Using a slotted spoon, transfer the mixture to the pan with the duck and stir in the parsley. Add the bay leaf and season to taste with salt and pepper. Pour in the wine and cook over a high heat, stirring occasionally, until reduced by half. Add the tomatoes, tomato purée and sugar and cook for a further 5 minutes. Pour in just enough water to cover and bring to the boil. Lower the heat, cover and simmer gently for 1 hour, until the duck is cooked through and tender.

3 Remove the pan from the heat and transfer the duck to a chopping board. Skim off the fat from the surface of the sauce and remove and discard the bay leaf. Remove and discard the skin from the duck and cut the meat off the bones, then dice. Return the duck meat to the pan and keep warm.

Bring a large saucepan of lightly salted water to the boil. Add the pasta, bring back to the boil and cook for 8–10 minutes, until tender but still firm to the bite. Drain and place in a serving dish and spoon the duck sauce over. Sprinkle generously with Parmesan cheese and serve immediately.

FISH & SEAFOOD

FISH SOUP WITH MACARONI

Serves: 6　　　**Prep: 20–25 mins**　　　**Cook: 30–35 mins**

Ingredients

2 tbsp olive oil

2 onions, sliced

1 garlic clove, finely chopped

1 litre/1¾ pints fish stock or water

400 g/14 oz canned chopped tomatoes

¼ tsp herbes de Provence

¼ tsp saffron threads

115 g/4 oz dried macaroni

18 live mussels, scrubbed and debearded

450 g/1 lb monkfish fillet, cut into chunks

225 g/8 oz raw prawns, peeled and deveined, tails left on

salt and pepper

Method

1 Heat the oil in a large, heavy-based saucepan. Add the onions and garlic and cook over a low heat, stirring occasionally, for 5 minutes, or until the onions have softened.

2 Add the fish stock with the tomatoes and their can juices, herbs, saffron and pasta and season to taste with salt and pepper. Bring to the boil, then cover and simmer for 15 minutes.

3 Discard any mussels with broken shells or any that refuse to close when tapped. Add the mussels, monkfish and prawns to the saucepan. Re-cover the saucepan and simmer for a further 5–10 minutes, until the mussels have opened, the prawns have changed colour and the fish is opaque and flakes easily. Discard any mussels that remain closed. Ladle the soup into warmed bowls and serve immediately.

★ Variation

For an extra special soup with a fragrant Mediterranean flavour, substitute 150 ml of the stock with white wine, and add a handful of basil in step 2.

SPAGHETTI & COD

Serves: 4   **Prep: 15–20 mins**   **Cook: 15 mins**

Ingredients

300 g/10½ oz dried spaghetti

200 ml/7 fl oz extra virgin olive oil

1 garlic clove, peeled

450 g/1 lb cherry tomatoes, halved

pinch of crushed dried chillies (optional)

600 g/1 lb 5 oz cod fillets, skinned and cut into small chunks

salt and pepper

Method

1 Bring a large saucepan of lightly salted water the boil. Add the pasta, bring back to the boil and cook for 8–10 minutes, until tender but still firm to the bite.

2 Meanwhile, put the oil into a large saucepan, add the garlic and cook over a low heat, stirri occasionally, for a few minutes until the garlic starts to brown, then remove and discard. Adc the tomatoes to the pan and season with salt. Increase the heat to high and cook, tossing ve occasionally, for 6–7 minutes until lightly browr and concentrated without disintegrating.

3 Add the chillies, if using, and the fish and cook stirring gently, for 1–2 minutes. Add a ladleful o the cooking water from the pasta and taste and adjust the seasoning, if necessary. Drain th pasta, tip it into the sauce and toss together. Remove from the heat, spoon into warmed bowls and serve immediately.

SICILIAN SWORDFISH PASTA

Serves: 4   **Prep: 20 mins**   **Cook: 30 mins**

Ingredients

1 tbsp olive oil

4 garlic cloves, peeled

1 onion, chopped

8 black olives, stoned and chopped

4 cornichons (small gherkins), chopped

2 tbsp capers in salt, rinsed and chopped

300 g/10½ oz dried spaghetti or linguine

400g/14 oz canned chopped tomatoes

450 g/1 lb swordfish, cut into small chunks

basil leaves, to garnish

salt and pepper

Method

1 Heat the oil in a deep frying pan and add the garlic. When the garlic begins to colour, remove and discard. Add the onion and cook over a heat, stirring occasionally, for 8–10 minutes until light golden. Stir in the olives, cornichons and capers, season to taste with salt and pepper and cook, stirring occasionally, for 5 minutes.

2 Meanwhile, bring a large saucepan of lightly salted water to the boil. Add the pasta, bring back to the boil and cook for 8–10 minutes, until tender but still firm to the bite.

3 Add the tomatoes to the frying pan, increase the heat to medium and bring to the boil, stirring occasionally, then reduce the heat and simmer for 5 minutes. Add the swordfish chunks, cover and simmer gently for a further 5 minutes.

4 Drain the pasta and tip into a warmed serving dish. Top with the swordfish sauce, garnish with the basil leaves and serve immediately.

FUSILLI WITH MONKFISH & BROCCOLI

Serves: 4　　　　**Prep: 20 mins**　　　　**Cook: 20 mins**

Ingredients

115 g/4 oz broccoli, separated into florets

3 tbsp olive oil

350 g/12 oz monkfish fillet, skinned and cut into bite-sized pieces

2 garlic cloves, crushed

125 ml/4 fl oz dry white wine

225 ml/8 fl oz double cream

400 g/14 oz dried fusilli

85 g/3 oz Gorgonzola cheese, diced

salt and pepper

Method

1 Separate the broccoli florets into small sprigs. Bring a saucepan of lightly salted water to the boil, add the broccoli and cook for 2 minutes. Drain and refresh under cold running water.

2 Heat the oil in a large, heavy-based frying pan. Add the monkfish and garlic and season to taste with salt and pepper. Cook, stirring frequently, for 5 minutes, or until the fish is opaque. Pour in the white wine and cream and cook, stirring occasionally, for 5 minutes, or until the fish is cooked through and the sauce has thickened. Stir in the broccoli florets.

3 Meanwhile, bring a large saucepan of lightly salted water to the boil. Add the pasta, return to the boil and cook for 8–10 minutes, or until tender but still firm to the bite. Drain and tip the pasta into the saucepan with the fish, add the cheese and toss lightly. Serve immediately.

LEMON PRAWNS WITH PASTA

Serves: 4   **Prep: 10 mins**   **Cook: 10 mins**

Ingredients

125 g/4½ oz butter

125 ml/4 fl oz olive oil

2 shallots, finely chopped

6 garlic cloves, finely chopped

¼ tsp dried red chilli flakes (optional)

finely grated rind of 1 large lemon

85 ml/3 fl oz dry white wine

2 tbsp lemon juice

600 g/1 lb 5 oz jumbo prawns, peeled and deveined

2 tbsp finely chopped fresh flat-leaf parsley

350 g/12 oz dried angel hair pasta

salt and pepper

Method

1 Melt the butter with the oil in a large frying p[an] over a medium–high heat. Add the shallots, garlic and chilli flakes (if using), and fry for 1–2 minutes, until the shallots are soft but not brow[n].

2 Stir in the lemon rind, wine and lemon juice, b[ring] to the boil and cook, stirring occasionally, for 2–3 minutes, until the sauce reduces slightly a[nd] the flavours blend. If the butter starts to brow[n,] immediately remove the pan from the heat.

3 Reduce the heat, add the prawns and cook, stirring occasionally, for 2–3 minutes, until they turn pink and curl. Stir in the parsley and seas[on] with salt and pepper.

4 Meanwhile, bring a large saucepan of lightly salted water to the boil. Add the pasta, bring back to the boil and cook for 2–4 minutes or, until tender and firm to the bite. Drain the pas[ta] well, then immediately add it to the pan with [the] prawns, using two forks to mix and blend all th[e] ingredients together.

5 Divide the pasta and prawns between warmed bowls, pour the cooking juices over and serve immediately.

LINGUINE WITH SARDINES

Serves: 4   **Prep: 25–30 mins**   **Cook: 15 mins**

Ingredients

8 sardines, filleted, washed and dried

4 tbsp olive oil

3 garlic cloves, sliced

1 tsp chilli flakes

1 fennel bulb, trimmed and thinly sliced

350 g/12 oz dried linguine

½ tsp finely grated lemon rind

1 tbsp lemon juice

2 tbsp toasted pine kernels

2 tbsp chopped fresh flat-leaf parsley

salt and pepper

Method

1 Roughly chop the sardines into large pieces a[nd] reserve.

2 Heat 2 tablespoons of the oil in a large frying pan over a medium–high heat and add the garlic and chilli flakes. Cook for 1 minute, then add the fennel. Cook, stirring occasionally, for 4–5 minutes, or until soft. Reduce the heat, add the sardine pieces and cook for a further 3–4 minutes.

3 Meanwhile, bring a large saucepan of lightly salted water to the boil. Add the pasta, bring back to the boil and cook for 8–10 minutes, un[til] tender but still firm to the bite. Drain thoroughly and return to the pan.

4 Add the lemon rind, lemon juice, pine kernels and parsley to the sardine mixture and toss. Season to taste with salt and pepper.

5 Add to the pasta with the remaining oil and toss. Transfer to a warmed serving dish and serve immediately.

FISH & SEAFOOD

SEA BASS WITH OLIVE SAUCE

erves: 4   **Prep: 15–20 mins**   **Cook: 30–35 mins**

Ingredients

50 g/1 lb dried rigatoni

1 tbsp olive oil

5 g/4 oz sea bass fillets

shredded leek and
dded carrot, to garnish

salt and pepper

Sauce

25 g/1 oz butter

4 shallots, chopped

2 tbsp capers

175 g/6 oz green olives,
stoned and chopped

tbsp balsamic vinegar

300 ml/10 fl oz fish stock

300 ml/10 fl oz
double cream

juice of 1 lemon

Method

1. To make the sauce, melt the butter in a frying pan. Add the shallots and cook over a low heat for 4 minutes. Add the capers and olives and cook for a further 3 minutes.

2. Stir in the balsamic vinegar and fish stock, bring to the boil and reduce by half. Add the cream, stirring constantly, and reduce again by half. Season to taste with salt and pepper and stir in the lemon juice. Remove the pan from the heat, set aside and keep warm.

3. Bring a large saucepan of lightly salted water to the boil. Add the pasta and olive oil and cook for 8–10 minutes, or until tender but still firm to the bite.

4. Meanwhile, lightly grill the sea bass fillets for 3–4 minutes on each side, until cooked through, but still moist and delicate.

5. Drain the pasta thoroughly and transfer to a large, warmed serving dish. Top the pasta with the fish and pour over the olive sauce. Garnish with shredded leek and shredded carrot and serve immediately.

FISH & SEAFOOD

CONCHIGLIE WITH SMOKED SALMON & SOURED CREAM

Serves: 4 **Prep: 15 mins** **Cook: 20 mins**

Ingredients

450 g/1 lb dried conchiglie

300 ml/10 fl oz
soured cream

2 tsp Dijon mustard

4 large spring onions,
sliced finely

225 g/8 oz smoked salmon,
cut into bite-sized pieces

finely grated rind of
½ lemon

salt and pepper

2 tbsp snipped fresh chives,
to garnish

Method

1 Bring a large, heavy-based saucepan of lightly salted water to the boil. Add the pasta, return to the boil and cook for 8–10 minutes, or until tender but still firm to the bite. Drain and return to the pan.

2 Add the soured cream, mustard, spring onions, smoked salmon and lemon rind to the pasta. S over a low heat until heated through. Season t taste with pepper.

3 Transfer to a warmed serving dish and garnish with the chives. Serve warm or at room temperature.

★ Variation

Try adding 115 g/4 oz sliced, fried mushrooms i step 2, seasoned with a handful of basil leaves

FARFALLE WITH SALMON & VEGETABLES

Serves: 2　　　　**Prep: 20–25 mins**　　　**Cook: 35–40 mins**

Ingredients

200 g/7 oz
asparagus, trimmed

pared zest of 1 lemon,
plus 1 tbsp lemon juice

1 tbsp olive oil

1 large courgette, thinly
sliced on the diagonal

150 g/5½ oz dried farfalle

100 g/3½ oz crème fraîche

55 g/2 oz baby
spinach leaves

200 g/7 oz cooked salmon
fillets, cut into
bite-sized pieces

salt and pepper

Method

1 Preheat a griddle pan until smoking hot. If the asparagus spears are plump, carefully slice the in half lengthways.

2 Mix the lemon juice and olive oil together. Add the asparagus and courgette. Season to taste with salt and pepper and toss together. Cook the vegetables in batches on the griddle pan for 2–3 minutes on each side until tender. Transf to a warmed plate and keep hot.

3 Bring a large saucepan of lightly salted water to the boil. Add the pasta, return to the boil and cook for 8–10 minutes, or until tender but still firm to the bite. Drain and put to one side. Heat the crème fraîche and lemon zest in the same saucepan until melted. Add the baby spinach leaves to the saucepan, followed by the pasta, chargrilled vegetables and salmon. Season to taste with salt and pepper and toss well. Serve immediately.

TAGLIATELLE WITH SMOKED SALMON & ROCKET

Serves: 4   **Prep: 15 mins**   **Cook: 15 mins**

Ingredients

350 g/12 oz dried tagliatelle

2 tbsp olive oil

1 garlic clove,
finely chopped

115 g/4 oz smoked salmon,
cut into thin strips

55 g/2 oz rocket

salt and pepper

Method

1 Bring a large saucepan of lightly salted water t
the boil. Add the pasta, bring back to the boil
and cook for 8–10 minutes, until tender but still
firm to the bite.

2 Just before the end of the cooking time, heat
the olive oil in a heavy-based frying pan. Add
the garlic and cook over a low heat, stirring
constantly, for 1 minute. Do not allow the garlic
brown or it will taste bitter.

3 Add the salmon and rocket. Season to taste w
pepper and cook, stirring constantly, for 1 minu
Remove the frying pan from the heat.

4 Drain the pasta and transfer to a warmed
serving dish. Add the smoked salmon and rock
mixture, toss lightly and serve immediately.

SALAD NIÇOISE

Serves: 4–6

Prep: 20 mins,
plus cooling

Cook: 22–26 mins

Ingredients

350 g/12 oz
dried conchiglie

2 tuna steaks, about
2 cm/¾ inch thick

olive oil, for brushing

250 g/9 oz French beans,
topped and tailed

shop-bought garlic
vinaigrette, to taste

2 hearts of lettuce,
leaves separated

3 large hard-boiled
eggs, halved

2 juicy tomatoes, cut
into wedges

50 g/1¾ oz anchovy fillets in
oil, drained

55 g/2 oz pitted black or
Niçoise olives

salt and pepper

Method

1 Bring a large saucepan of lightly salted water t
the boil. Add the pasta, bring back to the boil
and cook for 8–10 minutes, until tender but still
firm to the bite. Drain and refresh in cold water.

2 Heat a ridged cast-iron griddle pan over a high
heat. Brush the tuna steaks with oil on one side,
place oiled-side down on the hot pan and
chargrill for 2 minutes.

3 Lightly brush the top side of the tuna steaks with
a little more oil. Turn the tuna steaks over, then
season to taste with salt and pepper. Continue
chargrilling for a further 2 minutes for rare or up
to 4 minutes for well done. Leave to cool.

4 Meanwhile, bring a large saucepan of lightly
salted water to the boil. Add the beans and
return to the boil, then boil for 3 minutes. Drain
and immediately transfer to a large bowl. Pour
over the garlic vinaigrette and stir together.

5 To serve, line a serving dish with lettuce leaves
and add the cooled pasta. Lift the beans out
of the bowl, leaving the excess dressing behind
and pile them in the centre of the dish. Break
the tuna into large flakes and arrange it over th
beans.

6 Arrange the hard-boiled eggs, tomatoes,
anchovy fillets and olives on the dish. Serve.

FISH & SEAFOOD

SPAGHETTINI WITH QUICK TUNA SAUCE

Serves: 4   **Prep: 15–20 mins**   **Cook: 30 mins**

Ingredients

3 tbsp olive oil

4 tomatoes, peeled, deseeded and roughly chopped

115 g/4 oz mushrooms, sliced

1 tbsp chopped fresh basil

400 g/14 oz canned tuna, drained

100 ml/3½ fl oz fish stock or chicken stock

1 garlic clove, finely chopped

2 tsp chopped fresh marjoram

350 g/12 oz dried spaghettini

salt and pepper

115 g/4 oz freshly grated Parmesan cheese, to serve

Method

1 Heat the oil in a large frying pan. Add the tomatoes and cook over a low heat, stirring occasionally, for 15 minutes, or until pulpy. Add the mushrooms and cook, stirring occasionally, for a further 10 minutes. Stir in the basil, tuna, stock, garlic and marjoram and season to taste with salt and pepper. Cook over a low heat for 5 minutes, or until heated through.

2 Meanwhile, bring a large, heavy-based saucepan of lightly salted water to the boil. Add the pasta, return to the boil and cook for 8–10 minutes, or until tender but still firm to the bite.

3 Drain the pasta well, transfer to a warmed serving dish and spoon on the tuna mixture. Serve with grated Parmesan cheese.

FISH & SEAFOOD

CONCHIGLIE WITH TUNA, CAPERS & OLIVES

Serves: 4 **Prep: 15 mins** **Cook: 20–25 mins**

Ingredients

350 g/12 oz dried conchiglie

4 tbsp olive oil

4 tbsp butter

3 large garlic cloves, thinly sliced

200 g/7 oz canned tuna, drained and broken into chunks

2 tbsp lemon juice

1 tbsp capers, drained

8–12 black olives, stoned and sliced

salt

2 tbsp chopped fresh flat-leaf parsley, to serve

Method

1 Bring a large saucepan of lightly salted water to the boil. Add the pasta, bring back to the boil and cook for 8–10 minutes, or until tender but still firm to the bite. Drain and return to the pan.

2 Heat the olive oil and half the butter in a frying pan over a medium–low heat. Add the garlic and cook for a few seconds until just beginning to colour. Reduce the heat to low. Add the tuna, lemon juice, capers and olives. Stir gently until all the ingredients are heated through.

3 Transfer the pasta to a warmed serving dish. Pour the tuna mixture over the pasta. Add the parsley and remaining butter. Toss well to mix and serve immediately.

FISH & SEAFOOD

LINGUINE WITH CLAMS

Serves: 2–4 **Prep: 10 mins** **Cook: 10–15 mins**

Ingredients

200 g/7 oz dried linguine

3 tbsp extra virgin olive oil

4 garlic cloves, finely chopped

2 shallots, finely chopped

½ fresh red chilli, finely chopped

125 ml/4 fl oz white wine

1 kg/2 lb 4 oz fresh clams, tellines or cockles, cleaned

handful of fresh flat-leaf parsley, chopped

zest of 1 lemon

salt and pepper

Method

1 Bring a saucepan of lightly salted water to the boil. Add the pasta and cook for 8–10 minutes until tender but still firm to the bite. Drain and t with a splash of olive oil. Cover and keep warm

2 Discard any clams with broken shells or any th refuse to close when tapped. Meanwhile, add half the olive oil to a large saucepan with a lid and place over a high heat. Add the garlic, shallots and chilli and cook gently for 8–10 minutes until soft. Add the wine, bring to the bo and cook for 2 minutes. Add the clams, cover and cook for a further 2–5 minutes, or until all th clams have opened. Discard any clams which remain closed. Add the drained linguine, parsle lemon zest, the remaining olive oil and some sa and pepper and mix thoroughly.

3 Serve in warmed bowls, with another bowl for discarded shells.

FISH & SEAFOOD

SPAGHETTI ALLA PUTTANESCA

rves: 4   **Prep: 20 mins**   **Cook: 30 mins**

Ingredients

3 tbsp olive oil

2 garlic cloves, finely chopped

anchovy fillets, drained and chopped

140 g/5 oz black olives, stoned and chopped

1 tbsp capers, rinsed

g/1 lb plum tomatoes, peeled, deseeded and chopped

0 g/14 oz dried linguine

and cayenne pepper

2 tbsp chopped fresh -leaf parsley, to garnish

Method

1 Heat the oil in a heavy-based saucepan. Add the garlic and cook over a low heat, stirring frequently, for 2 minutes. Add the anchovies and mash them to a pulp with a fork.

2 Add the olives, capers and tomatoes and season to taste with cayenne pepper. Cover and simmer for 25 minutes.

3 Meanwhile, bring a saucepan of lightly salted water to the boil. Add the pasta, bring back to the boil and cook for 8–10 minutes, until tender but still firm to the bite.

4 Drain the pasta and transfer to a warmed serving dish. Spoon the anchovy sauce over the pasta and toss.

5 Garnish with chopped parsley and serve immediately.

FISH & SEAFOOD

SPAGHETTI WITH CRAB

Serves: 4   **Prep: 20 mins**   **Cook: 15 mins**

Ingredients

1 dressed crab, about 450 g/1 lb including the shell

350 g/12 oz dried spaghetti

6 tbsp extra virgin olive oil

1 fresh red chilli, deseeded and finely chopped

2 garlic cloves, finely chopped

3 tbsp chopped fresh flat-leaf parsley

2 tbsp lemon juice

1 tsp finely grated lemon rind

salt and pepper

lemon wedges, to garnish

Method

1 Using a sharp knife, scoop the meat from the crab shell into a bowl. Mix the white and brown meat together lightly and reserve.

2 Bring a large saucepan of lightly salted water to the boil. Add the pasta, bring back to the boil and cook for 8–10 minutes, or until tender but still firm to the bite. Drain thoroughly and return to the pan.

3 Meanwhile, heat 2 tablespoons of the oil in a frying pan over a low heat. Add the chilli and garlic and cook for 30 seconds, then add the crabmeat, parsley, lemon juice and rind. Cook 1 minute, until the crab is just heated through.

4 Add the crab mixture to the pasta with the remaining oil and season to taste with salt and pepper. Toss together thoroughly and transfer to a large, warmed serving dish and garnish with a few lemon wedges. Serve immediately.

PASTA SALAD WITH MELON & PRAWNS

Serves: 6   **Prep: 30–35 mins**   **Cook: 15 mins**

Ingredients

225 g/8 oz dried green fusilli

5 tbsp extra virgin olive oil

450 g/1 lb cooked prawns

1 Charentais melon

1 Galia melon

1 tbsp red wine vinegar

1 tsp Dijon mustard

pinch of caster sugar

1 tbsp chopped fresh
flat-leaf parsley

1 tbsp chopped fresh basil,
plus extra sprigs to garnish

1 oakleaf or quattro
stagioni lettuce, shredded

salt and pepper

Method

1 Bring a large saucepan of lightly salted water
the boil. Add the pasta, bring back to the boil
and cook for 8–10 minutes, until tender but still
firm to the bite. Drain, toss with 1 tablespoon c
the oil and leave to cool.

2 Meanwhile, peel and devein the prawns, then
place them in a large bowl. Halve both the
melons and scoop out the seeds with a spoor
Using a melon baller or teaspoon, scoop out
balls of the flesh and add them to the prawns

3 Whisk together the remaining oil, the vinegar,
mustard, sugar, parsley and basil in a small bov
Season to taste with salt and pepper. Add the
cooled pasta to the prawn and melon mixture
and toss lightly to mix, then pour in the dressing
and toss again. Cover with clingfilm and chill in
the refrigerator for 30 minutes.

4 Make a bed of shredded lettuce on a serving
plate. Spoon the pasta salad on top, garnish w
basil sprigs and serve immediately.

SPRINGTIME PASTA

Serves: 4   **Prep: 30–35 mins**   **Cook: 20 mins**

Ingredients

2 tbsp lemon juice

4 baby globe artichokes

7 tbsp olive oil

2 shallots, finely chopped

2 garlic cloves, finely chopped

2 tbsp chopped fresh flat-leaf parsley

2 tbsp chopped fresh mint

350 g/12 oz dried rigatoni

25 g/1 oz unsalted butter

12 large raw prawns, peeled and deveined

salt and pepper

Method

1 Fill a bowl with cold water and add the lemon juice. Prepare the artichokes one at a time. Cut off the stems and trim away any tough outer leaves. Cut across the tops of the leaves. Slice in half lengthways and remove the central fibrous chokes, then cut lengthways into 5-mm/¼-inch thick slices. Immediately place the slices in the bowl of acidulated water.

2 Heat 5 tablespoons of the oil in a heavy-based frying pan. Drain the artichoke slices and pat dry with kitchen paper. Add them to the frying pan with the shallots, garlic, parsley and mint and cook over a low heat, stirring frequently, for 10–12 minutes, until tender.

3 Meanwhile, bring a large saucepan of lightly salted water to the boil. Add the pasta, bring back to the boil and cook for 8–10 minutes, until tender but still firm to the bite.

4 Melt the butter in a small frying pan and add the prawns. Cook, stirring occasionally, for 2–3 minutes, until opaque and firm to the touch. Season to taste with salt and pepper.

5 Drain the pasta and tip it into a bowl. Add the remaining oil and toss. Add the artichoke mixture and the prawns and toss again. Spoon into warmed bowls and serve immediately.

FETTUCCINE & PRAWN PARCELS

Serves: 4   **Prep: 25–30 mins**   **Cook: 20–25 mins**

Ingredients

450 g/1 lb dried fettuccine

150 ml/5 fl oz pesto

4 tsp extra virgin olive oil

750 g/1 lb 10 oz large raw prawns, peeled and deveined

2 garlic cloves, crushed

125 ml/4 fl oz dry white wine

salt and pepper

Method

1 Preheat the oven to 200°C/400°F/Gas Mark 6. Cut out 4 x 30-cm/12-inch squares of greaseproof paper. Bring a large saucepan of lightly salted water to the boil. Add the pasta, bring back to the boil and cook for 2–3 minutes or until just softened. Drain and reserve.

2 Mix the fettuccine and half of the pesto together in a bowl. Spread out the paper squares and place 1 teaspoon of oil in the centre of each. Divide the fettuccine between the squares, then divide the prawns and place on top of the fettuccine. Mix the remaining pesto and the garlic together and spoon it over the prawns. Season each parcel to taste with salt and pepper and sprinkle with the white wine. Dampen the edges of the greaseproof paper and wrap the parcels loosely, twisting the edges to seal.

3 Place the parcels on a baking sheet and bake in the preheated oven for 10–15 minutes. Transfer the parcels to warmed plates and serve immediately.

FISH & SEAFOOD

GARLIC PRAWNS WITH ANGEL HAIR PASTA

Serves: 4　　　　**Prep: 30 mins**　　　　**Cook: 40 mins**

Ingredients

500 g/1 lb 2 oz raw tiger prawns

1 avocado

2 tbsp lemon juice

4 tbsp olive oil

1 onion, finely chopped

350 ml/12 fl oz dry white wine

1 bouquet garni

300 g/10½ oz dried angel hair pasta

3 large garlic cloves, finely chopped

salt and pepper

Method

1 Peel the prawns, reserving the heads and shells. Cut along the back of each prawn and remove the black vein. Peel, stone and slice the avocado, put into a bowl and toss with the lemon juice.

2 Heat half the oil in a saucepan, add the onion and cook over a low heat, stirring occasionally, for 5 minutes. Add the prawn heads and shells and cook, mashing with a wooden spoon, for 5 minutes, then add the wine and bouquet garni. Increase the heat to medium and bring to the boil. Reduce the heat and simmer for 20 minutes.

3 Meanwhile, bring a large saucepan of lightly salted water to the boil. Add the pasta, bring back to the boil and cook for 3 minutes. Remove from the heat, drain and set aside.

4 Remove and discard the bouquet garni. Transfer the prawn shell mixture to a food processor or blender and process until combined, then strain into a clean saucepan. Bring to the boil, then add the pasta and cook for a few more minutes until the pasta is tender but still firm to the bite.

5 Meanwhile, heat the remaining oil in a frying pan over a medium heat. Add the prawns and cook, stirring frequently, for 2–3 minutes until opaque and firm to the touch. Add the garlic and cook,

FISH & SEAFOOD

stirring frequently for a further minute. Season to taste with salt and pepper and remove from the heat.

Drain the pasta, toss with the avocado and transfer to a serving dish. Top with the prawns and serve immediately.

TAGLIATELLE WITH PRAWNS & SCALLOPS

Serves: 6   **Prep: 20–25 mins**   **Cook: 40 mins**

Ingredients

450 g/1 lb raw prawns

25 g/1 oz butter

2 shallots, finely chopped

225 ml/8 fl oz dry white vermouth

350 ml/12 fl oz water

450 g/1 lb dried tagliatelle

2 tbsp olive oil

450 g/1 lb prepared scallops

2 tbsp snipped fresh chives, plus chive flowers, to garnish

salt and pepper

Method

1 Peel and devein the prawns, reserving the she
Melt the butter in a heavy-based frying pan. A
the shallots and cook over a low heat, stirring
occasionally, for 5 minutes, or until softened. Ac
the prawn shells and cook, stirring constantly, fc
1 minute. Pour in the vermouth and cook, stirrin
constantly, for 1 minute. Add the water, bring tc
the boil, then reduce the heat and simmer for
10 minutes, or until the liquid has reduced by he
Remove the frying pan from the heat.

2 Bring a large saucepan of lightly salted water
to the boil. Add the pasta, return to the boil and
cook for 8–10 minutes, or until tender but still firr
to the bite.

3 Meanwhile, heat the olive oil in a separate
heavy-based frying pan. Add the scallops and
prawns and cook, stirring frequently, for 2 minute
or until the scallops are opaque and the prawn:
turn pink. Strain the prawn-shell stock into the
frying pan. Drain the pasta and add to the fryin
pan with the chives and season to taste with
salt and pepper. Toss well over a low heat for
1 minute, then serve immediately, garnished wit
a chive flower.

SCALLOP SOUP WITH PASTA

Serves: 6 **Prep: 20 mins** **Cook: 15 mins**

Ingredients

500 g/1 lb 2 oz
shelled scallops

350 ml/12 fl oz milk

1.5 litres/2¾ pints
vegetable stock

250 g/9 oz frozen petits pois

175 g/6 oz tagliatelle

70 g/2½ oz butter

2 spring onions,
finely chopped

175 ml/6 fl oz dry white wine

3 slices of prosciutto, cut
into thin strips

salt and pepper

chopped fresh flat-leaf
parsley, to garnish

Method

1 Slice the scallops in half horizontally and seas
with salt and pepper.

2 Pour the milk and stock into a saucepan, ad
pinch of salt and bring to the boil. Add the p
pois and pasta, bring back to the boil and co
for 8–10 minutes, until the tagliatelle is tender
still firm to the bite.

3 Meanwhile, melt the butter in a frying pan. A
the spring onions and cook over a low heat,
stirring occasionally, for 3 minutes. Add the
scallops and cook for 45 seconds on each si
Pour in the wine, add the prosciutto and coo
2–3 minutes.

4 Stir the scallop mixture into the soup, taste ar
adjust the seasoning, if necessary, and garnis
with the parsley. Serve immediately.

PAPPARDELLE WITH SCALLOPS & PORCINI

Serves: 4

Prep: 20 mins, plus soaking

Cook: 20 mins

Ingredients

25 g/1 oz dried porcini mushrooms

500 ml/18 fl oz hot water

3 tbsp olive oil

3 tbsp butter

350 g/12 oz prepared scallops, sliced

2 garlic cloves, very finely chopped

2 tbsp lemon juice

250 ml/9 fl oz double cream

350 g/12 oz dried pappardelle

salt and pepper

2 tbsp chopped fresh flat-leaf parsley, to garnish

Method

1 Put the porcini and hot water in a bowl. Leave to soak for 20 minutes. Strain the mushrooms, reserving the soaking water, and roughly chop Line a sieve with two pieces of kitchen paper and strain the mushroom water into a bowl.

2 Heat the oil and butter in a large frying pan ov a medium heat. Add the scallops and cook fo 2 minutes until just golden. Add the garlic and mushrooms, then cook for another minute.

3 Stir in the lemon juice, cream and 125 ml/4 fl o of the mushroom water. Bring to the boil, then simmer over a medium heat for 2–3 minutes, stirring constantly, until the liquid is reduced by half. Season to taste with salt and pepper. Remove from the heat.

4 Meanwhile, bring a large, heavy-based saucepan of lightly salted water to the boil. Ac the pasta, bring back to the boil and cook for 8–10 minutes, or until tender but still firm to the bite. Drain and transfer to a warmed serving d Briefly reheat the sauce and pour over the pas Garnish with the parsley and toss well to mix. Serve immediately.

FISH & SEAFOOD

MACARONI WITH SCALLOPS & PINE KERNELS

Serves: 4   **Prep: 15 mins**   **Cook: 15 mins**

Ingredients

400 g/14 oz dried long
macaroni

4 tbsp olive oil

1 garlic clove,
finely chopped

55 g/2 oz pine kernels

8 large prepared
scallops, sliced

salt and pepper

sp shredded fresh basil
leaves, to garnish

Method

1. Bring a large, heavy-based saucepan of lightly salted water to the boil. Add the pasta, return to the boil and cook for 8–10 minutes, or until tender but still firm to the bite.

2. About 5 minutes before the pasta is ready, heat the oil in a frying pan. Add the garlic and cook for 1–2 minutes until softened but not browned. Add the pine kernels and cook until browned. Stir in the scallops and cook until just opaque. Season to taste with salt and pepper.

3. When the pasta is cooked, drain and return to the saucepan. Add the scallops, pine kernels, garlic and the juices in the frying pan to the pasta and toss together. Serve garnished with the shredded basil leaves.

BAKED SCALLOPS WITH PASTA IN SHELLS

Serves: 4   **Prep: 35 mins**   **Cook: 25–30 mins**

Ingredients

12 scallops

3 tbsp olive oil

350 g/12 oz dried conchiglie

150 ml/5 fl oz fresh fish stock

1 onion, chopped

juice and finely grated rind of 2 lemons

150 ml/5 fl oz double cream

225 g/8 oz grated Cheddar cheese

salt and pepper

crusty brown bread, to serve

Method

1 Preheat the oven to 180°C/350°F/Gas Mark 4. Remove the scallops from their shells. Scrape the skirt and the black intestinal thread. Reserve the white part (the flesh) and the orange part (the coral or roe). Very carefully ease the flesh and coral from the shell with a short, but very strong knife.

2 Wash the shells thoroughly and dry them well. Put the shells on a baking tray, sprinkle lightly 2 tablespoons of the olive oil and set aside.

3 Meanwhile, bring a large saucepan of lightly salted water to the boil. Add the conchiglie and remaining olive oil and cook for 8–10 minutes or until tender but still firm to the bite. Drain and spoon about 25 g/1 oz of pasta into each scallop shell.

4 Put the scallops, fish stock and onion in an ovenproof dish and season to taste with pepper. Cover with foil and bake in the preheated oven for 8 minutes.

5 Remove the dish from the oven. Remove the foil then use a perforated spoon to transfer the scallops to the shells. Add 1 tbsp of the cooking liquid to each shell, together with a drizzle of lemon juice, a little lemon rind and cream, and top with the Cheddar cheese.

FISH & SEAFOOD

Increase the oven temperature to 230°C/450°F/Gas Mark 8 and return the scallops to the oven for a further 4 minutes.

Serve the scallops in their shells with crusty brown bread.

FARFALLINI BUTTERED LOBSTER

Serves: 4　　　**Prep: 35 mins**　　　**Cook: 20 mins**

Ingredients

2 lobsters (about 700 g/1 lb 9 oz each), split into halves

juice and grated rind of 1 lemon

115 g/4 oz butter

4 tbsp fresh white breadcrumbs

2 tbsp brandy

5 tbsp double cream or crème fraîche

450 g/1 lb dried farfallini

55 g/2 oz freshly grated Parmesan cheese

salt and pepper

lemon wedges and fresh dill sprigs, to garnish

Method

1 Preheat the oven to 160°C/325°F/Gas Mark 3. Discard the stomach sac, vein and gills from each lobster. Remove the meat from the tail and chop. Crack the claws and legs, remove the meat and chop. Transfer the meat to a bowl and add the lemon juice and lemon rind. Clean the shells and place in the oven to dry out.

2 Melt 25 g/1 oz of the butter in a frying pan. Add the breadcrumbs and cook for 3 minutes, until crisp and golden brown. Melt the remaining butter in a separate saucepan. Add the lobster meat and heat through gently. Add the brandy and cook for a further 3 minutes, then add the cream and season to taste with salt and pepper.

3 Meanwhile, bring a large saucepan of lightly salted water to the boil. Add the pasta, bring back to the boil and cook for 8–10 minutes, until tender but still firm to the bite. Drain and spoon the pasta into the clean lobster shells.

4 Preheat the grill to medium. Spoon the buttered lobster on top of the pasta and sprinkle with a little Parmesan cheese and the breadcrumbs. Grill for 2–3 minutes, or until golden brown. Transfer the lobster shells to a warmed plate, garnish with the lemon wedges and dill sprigs and serve immediately.

CLAM & PASTA SOUP

Serves: 6   **Prep: 20–25 mins**   **Cook: 35 mins**

Ingredients

3 tbsp olive oil

1 Spanish onion, finely chopped

3 cloves garlic, finely chopped

600 g/1 lb 5 oz canned chopped tomatoes

2 tbsp tomato purée

2 tsp sugar

1 tsp dried oregano

1 litre/1¾ pints vegetable stock

500 g/1 lb 2 oz live clams, scrubbed

175 ml/6 fl oz dry white wine

85 g/3 oz dried conchigliette

3 tbsp chopped fresh flat-leaf parsley

salt and pepper

Method

1 Heat the oil in a large saucepan. Add the onion and garlic and cook over a low heat, stirring occasionally, for 5 minutes, until softened. Add the tomatoes, tomato purée, sugar, oregano and stock and season with salt and pepper. Mix well and bring to the boil, then reduce the heat, cover and simmer, stirring occasionally, for 5 minutes.

2 Discard any clams with broken shells and any that refuse to close when tapped. Put the clams into a saucepan, pour in the wine, cover and cook over a high heat, shaking the pan occasionally, for 3–5 minutes.

3 Remove the clams from the heat and remove from the liquid with a slotted spoon. Reserve the cooking liquid. Discard any clams that remain closed and remove the remainder from the half shells. Strain the reserved cooking liquid into a bowl and set aside.

4 Add the pasta to the soup and simmer, uncovered, for 10 minutes. Add the cooked clams and the reserved cooking liquid. Stir well and heat gently for 4–5 minutes; do not allow the soup to come back to the boil. Taste and adjust the seasoning, if necessary, stir in the parsley and serve immediately.

FETTUCCINE WITH LEMON PEPPER SEAFOOD

Serves: 4　　　　**Prep: 15 mins**　　　　**Cook: 20 mins**

Ingredients

5 tbsp lemon pepper oil,
plus extra to serve

6 garlic cloves, crushed

675 g/1 lb 8 oz mixed
seafood (prawns,
squid, mussels)

dash of vodka

125 ml/4 fl oz white wine

1 sprig tarragon, leaves only

dash of salt

450 g/1 lb fettuccine

chopped flat-leaf parsley,
to garnish

Method

1 Heat a wok or deep frying pan and add the lemon pepper oil. When the oil is hot, add the garlic and seafood. Stir for 1 minute. Add a dash of vodka, the white wine, tarragon leaves and salt. Keep stirring until the seafood is cooked through.

2 Bring a large saucepan of lightly salted water to boil over a medium heat. Add the pasta and cook for 8–10 minutes, or until tender but still firm to the bite. Drain and add the pasta to the seafood mixture. Toss well and serve immediately on warmed plates. Drizzle more lemon pepper oil on top to serve and garnish with the chopped parsley.

★ Variation

Try substituting the prawns for crabmeat or scallops, or create your own mix using your favourite types of seafood.

FILLED & BAKED

SPINACH & TOMATO TORTELLINI SOUP

Serves: 4   **Prep: 15 mins**   **Cook: 25 mins**

Ingredients

4 tbsp olive oil

1 onion, thinly sliced

2 garlic cloves, finely chopped

850 ml/1½ pints chicken stock

500 g/1 lb 2 oz fresh or frozen chicken or pork tortellini

400 g/14 oz canned chopped tomatoes

1 tbsp sun-dried tomato purée

400 g/14 oz canned borlotti beans, drained and rinsed

350 g/12 oz spinach, coarse stalks removed, rinsed and drained

2 tbsp chopped fresh flat-leaf parsley

salt and pepper

freshly grated Parmesan cheese, to serve

Method

1 Heat the oil in a saucepan, add the onion and garlic and cook over a low heat, stirring occasionally, for 5 minutes until soft. Pour in the stock, increase the heat to medium and bring to the boil.

2 Add the tortellini and cook for 5 minutes, then reduce the heat, add the tomatoes and their can juices, tomato purée and beans and season to taste with salt and pepper. Reduce the heat and simmer for a further 5 minutes. Stir in the spinach and parsley and cook for 1–2 minutes until the spinach is just wilted. Remove from the heat and serve immediately, with the cheese separately.

★ Variation

For the perfect dish, try creating home-made tortellini with your favourite filling instead of using pre-made pasta.

WARM RAVIOLI SALAD

Serves: 4 **Prep: 20–25 mins** **Cook: 15 mins**

Ingredients

125 ml/4 fl oz olive oil

2 tbsp balsamic vinegar

1 tsp Dijon mustard

1 tsp sugar

½ small cucumber, peeled

225 g/8 oz mixed lettuce leaves

115 g/4 oz rocket

1 head chicory, sliced

3 tbsp mixed chopped herbs, such as parsley, thyme and coriander

2 tomatoes, cut into wedges

2 red peppers or yellow peppers preserved in oil, drained and sliced

20 fresh beef ravioli

25 g/1 oz butter

salt and pepper

Method

1 Whisk 100 ml/3½ fl oz of the oil, the vinegar, mustard and sugar together in a bowl and season to taste with salt and pepper. Set aside.

2 Halve the cucumber lengthways and scoop out the seeds, then slice. Tear the lettuce and rocket leaves into small pieces. Put the cucumber, lettuce, rocket, chicory, herbs, tomatoes and preserved peppers into a bowl and set aside.

3 Bring a large saucepan of lightly salted water to the boil. Add the ravioli and cook according to the packet instructions, then drain. Melt the butter with the remaining oil in a frying pan. Add the ravioli and cook over a medium heat, turning carefully once or twice, for 5 minutes until golden on both sides. Remove the pan from the heat.

4 Pour the dressing over the salad and toss, then divide between individual serving plates. Top with the ravioli and serve immediately.

HAM & RICOTTA CANNELLONI

Serves: 4   **Prep: 10 mins**   **Cook: 1 hour 5 mins**

Ingredients

2 tbsp olive oil

2 onions, chopped

2 garlic cloves, finely chopped

1 tbsp shredded fresh basil

800 g/1 lb 12 oz canned chopped tomatoes

1 tbsp tomato purée

10–12 dried cannelloni tubes

butter, for greasing

225 g/8 oz ricotta cheese

115 g/4 oz cooked ham, diced

1 egg

55 g/2 oz freshly grated pecorino cheese

salt and pepper

Method

1 Preheat the oven to 180°C/350°F/Gas Mark 4. Heat the oil in a large heavy-based frying pan. Add the onions and garlic and cook over a low heat, stirring occasionally, for 5 minutes, or until the onion is softened. Add the basil, tomatoes and their can juices and tomato purée and season to taste with salt and pepper. Reduce the heat and simmer for 30 minutes, or until thickened.

2 Meanwhile, bring a large saucepan of lightly salted water to the boil. Add the cannelloni tubes, return to the boil and cook for 8–10 minutes, or until tender but still firm to the bite. Using a slotted spoon, transfer the cannelloni tubes to a large plate and pat dry with kitchen paper.

3 Grease a large, shallow ovenproof dish with butter. Mix the ricotta, ham and egg together in a bowl and season to taste with salt and pepper. Using a teaspoon, fill the cannelloni tubes with the ricotta mixture and place in a single layer in the dish. Pour the tomato sauce over the cannelloni and sprinkle with the grated pecorino cheese. Bake in the preheated oven for 30 minutes, or until golden brown. Serve immediately.

FILLED & BAKED

MIXED VEGETABLE AGNOLOTTI

Serves: 4

Prep: 35–40 mins, plus resting

Cook: 55 mins

Ingredients

Pasta dough

200 g/7 oz white bread flour

1 tsp salt

2 eggs, lightly beaten

1 tbsp olive oil

Filling

125 ml/4 fl oz olive oil

1 red onion, chopped

3 garlic cloves, chopped

2 large aubergines, cut into chunks

3 large courgettes, cut into chunks

6 beefsteak tomatoes, peeled, deseeded and chopped

1 large green pepper, deseeded and diced

1 large red pepper, deseeded and diced

1 tbsp sun-dried tomato purée

1 tbsp shredded fresh basil

salt and pepper

butter, for greasing

plain flour, for dusting

85 g/3 oz freshly grated Parmesan cheese

mixed salad leaves, to serve

Method

1 To make the pasta dough, sift the flour into a food processor. Add the salt, eggs and olive oil and process until the dough begins to come together. Knead on a lightly floured board until smooth. Cover and let rest for 30 minutes.

2 To make the filling, heat the olive oil in a large, heavy-based saucepan. Add the onion and garlic and cook over a low heat, stirring occasionally, for 5 minutes, or until softened. Add the aubergine, courgettes, tomatoes, green and red peppers, sun-dried tomato purée and basil. Season with salt and pepper, cover and simmer gently, stirring occasionally, for 20 minutes.

3 Lightly grease an ovenproof dish with butter. Roll out the pasta dough on a lightly floured board and stamp out 7.5-cm/3-inch circles with a plain cutter. Place a spoonful of the vegetable filling on one side of each circle. Dampen the edges slightly and fold the pasta circles over, pressing together to seal.

4 Preheat the oven to 200°C/400°F/Gas Mark 6. Bring a large pan of lightly salted water to the boil. Add the agnolotti, return to the boil and cook for 3–4 minutes. Remove with a slotted spoon, drain and transfer to the dish. Sprinkle with the Parmesan and bake in the preheated oven for 20 minutes. Serve with salad leaves.

FILLED & BAKED

LAYERED SALMON & PRAWN SPAGHETTI

Serves: 6 **Prep: 20–25 mins** **Cook: 30 mins**

Ingredients

350 g/12 oz dried spaghetti

70 g/2½ oz butter, plus extra for greasing

200 g/7 oz smoked salmon, cut into strips

280 g/10 oz large cooked prawns, peeled and deveined

300 ml/10 fl oz béchamel sauce

115 g/4 oz freshly grated Parmesan cheese

salt

rocket, to garnish

Method

1 Preheat the oven to 180°C/350°F/Gas Mark 4. Grease a large ovenproof dish with butter and set aside.

2 Bring a large saucepan of lightly salted water to the boil. Add the pasta, bring back to the boil and cook for 8–10 minutes, until tender but still firm to the bite. Drain well, return to the saucepan, add 55 g/2 oz of the butter and toss well.

3 Spoon half the spaghetti into the prepared dish, cover with the strips of smoked salmon, then top with the prawns. Pour over half the béchamel sauce and sprinkle with half the cheese. Add the rest of the spaghetti, cover with the remaining sauce and sprinkle with the remaining cheese. Dice the reserved butter and dot it over the surface.

4 Bake in the preheated oven for 15 minutes, until golden and bubbling. Serve immediately, garnished with rocket.

KALE & RICOTTA CANNELLONI

Serves: 4   **Prep: 35–40 mins**   **Cook: 1 hour 10 mins–1 hour 20 mins**

Ingredients

350 g/12 oz kale leaves

250 g/9 oz ricotta cheese

finely grated rind of 1 lemon

1 tsp fresh thyme leaves

¼ tsp ground nutmeg

40 g/1½ oz freshly grated Parmesan cheese

handful of basil leaves, torn

12 dried no pre-cook cannelloni tubes

Sauce

800 g/1 lb 12 oz canned chopped tomatoes

2 onions, quartered

55 g/2 oz butter

225 ml/8 fl oz hot chicken stock or vegetable stock

salt and pepper

Method

1 To make the sauce, put the tomatoes, onions and butter in a saucepan over a medium heat. Simmer, uncovered, for 45 minutes, stirring occasionally. Strain to remove the onion, then pour back into the pan. Stir in the stock, season to taste with salt and pepper, then set aside and keep warm.

2 Meanwhile, stack the kale leaves and slice into ribbons. Steam for 5 minutes until just tender. Drain and rinse under cold running water, squeezing hard with your hands to press out as much liquid as possible.

3 Mix the kale with the ricotta cheese, lemon rind thyme and nutmeg. Add half the Parmesan cheese and the basil and season to taste with salt and pepper. Stuff the mixture into the cannelloni tubes, packing it in well.

4 Preheat the oven to 180°C/350°F/Gas Mark 4.

5 Spoon half the sauce over the base of an ovenproof dish large enough to take the tubes comfortably in a single layer. Arrange the tubes on top and spoon over the remaining sauce. Scatter with the remaining Parmesan cheese.

6 Cover with foil and bake in the preheated oven for 25–35 minutes until thoroughly heated through. Serve hot.

FILLED & BAKED

HOT TOMATO & CONCHIGLIE GRATIN

Serves: 4   **Prep: 15 mins**   **Cook: 18–22 mins**

Ingredients

1 onion, chopped

400 g/14 oz canned chopped tomatoes

225 ml/8 fl oz milk

2 red chillies, deseeded and finely chopped

1 garlic clove, finely chopped

pinch of ground coriander

280 g/10 oz dried conchiglie

85 g/3 oz Gruyère cheese, grated

salt and pepper

Method

1 Put the onion, tomatoes and milk in a large, heavy-based saucepan and bring just to the boil. Add the chillies, garlic, coriander and pasta, season with salt and pepper and cook over a medium heat, stirring frequently, for 2–3 minutes.

2 Add just enough water to cover and cook, stirring frequently, for 8–10 minutes, until the pasta is tender but still firm to the bite. Meanwhile, preheat the grill.

3 Spoon the pasta mixture into individual flameproof dishes and sprinkle evenly with the cheese. Place under the grill for 3–4 minutes, until the cheese has melted. Serve immediately.

FILLED & BAKED

CHICKEN RAVIOLI IN TARRAGON BROTH

Serves: 6

Prep: 40–45 mins, plus chilling

Cook: 35–40 mins

Ingredients

2 litres/3½ pints chicken stock

2 tbsp finely chopped fresh tarragon leaves

freshly grated Parmesan cheese, to serve

Pasta dough

125 g/4½ oz flour, plus extra for dusting

2 tbsp fresh tarragon leaves, stems removed

1 egg

1 egg, separated

1 tsp extra virgin olive oil

2–3 tbsp water

pinch of salt

Filling

200 g/7 oz cooked chicken, coarsely chopped

½ tsp grated lemon rind

2 tbsp chopped mixed fresh tarragon, chives and parsley

4 tbsp whipping cream

salt and pepper

Method

1 To make the pasta, combine the flour, tarragon and salt in a food processor or blender. Beat together the egg, egg yolk, oil and 2 tablespoons of water. With the machine running, pour in the egg mixture and process until it forms a ball. Wrap and chill for 30 minutes. Reserve the egg white.

2 To make the filling, put the chicken, lemon rind and mixed herbs in a food processor or blender and season to taste with salt and pepper. Chop finely. Do not overprocess. Scrape into a bowl and stir in the cream.

3 Divide the pasta dough in half. Cover one half and roll out the other half on a floured surface to less than 1.5 mm/¹/₁₆ inch. Cut out rectangles measuring about 10 x 5 cm/4 x 2 inches. Place a teaspoon of filling on one half of each rectangle. Brush the edges with egg white and fold in half. Press the edges to seal. Arrange on a baking sheet dusted with flour. Repeat with the remaining dough. Allow the ravioli to dry for about 15 minutes or chill for 1–2 hours in the refrigerator.

4 Bring a large saucepan of water to the boil. Drop in half of the ravioli and cook for 12–15 minutes, or until just tender. Drain on a tea towel while cooking the remainder.

FILLED & BAKED

Meanwhile, put the stock and tarragon in a large saucepan. Bring to the
oil, then cover and simmer for 15 minutes. Add the ravioli and simmer for
further 5 minutes. Ladle into warmed bowls and serve immediately with
armesan cheese.

MUSHROOM CANNELLONI

Serves: 4 **Prep: 35 mins** **Cook: 55 mins– 1 hour**

Ingredients

12 dried cannelloni tubes

6 tbsp olive oil, plus extra for brushing

1 onion, finely chopped

2 garlic cloves, finely chopped

800 g/1 lb 12 oz canned chopped tomatoes

1 tbsp tomato purée

8 black olives, stoned and chopped

25 g/1 oz butter

450 g/1 lb wild mushrooms, finely chopped

85 g/3 oz fresh breadcrumbs

150 ml/5 fl oz milk

225 g/8 oz ricotta cheese

6 tbsp freshly grated Parmesan cheese

2 tbsp pine kernels

2 tbsp flaked almonds

salt and pepper

Method

1 Preheat the oven to 190°C/375°F/Gas Mark 5. Bring a large saucepan of lightly salted water to the boil. Add the cannelloni tubes, return to the boil and cook for 8–10 minutes, or until tender but still firm to the bite. With a slotted spoon, transfer the cannelloni tubes to a plate and pat dry. Brush a large ovenproof dish with oil.

2 Heat 2 tablespoons of the oil in a frying pan, add the onion and half the garlic and cook over a low heat for 5 minutes, or until softened. Add the tomatoes and their can juices, tomato purée and olives and season to taste with salt and pepper. Bring to the boil and cook for 3–4 minutes. Pour the sauce into the ovenproof dish.

3 To make the filling, melt the butter in a heavy-based frying pan. Add the mushrooms and remaining garlic and cook over a medium heat, stirring frequently, for 3–5 minutes, or until tender.

4 Remove the frying pan from the heat. Mix the breadcrumbs, milk and remaining oil together in a large bowl, then stir in the ricotta, the mushroom mixture and 4 tablespoons of the Parmesan cheese. Season to taste with salt and pepper.

Fill the cannelloni tubes with the mushroom mixture and place them in the prepared dish. Brush with oil and sprinkle with the remaining Parmesan cheese, the pine kernels and almonds. Bake in the preheated oven for 25 minutes until golden and bubbling. Serve immediately.

CHICKEN & LEEK LASAGNE

Serves: 2

Prep: 25–30 mins, plus cooling

Cook: 45–50 mins

Ingredients

55 g/2 oz butter, plus extra for greasing

1 tbsp vegetable oil

1 large or 2 medium leeks, thinly sliced

2 skinless, boneless chicken breasts, about 115 g/4 oz each

2 tbsp flour

200 ml/7 fl oz milk

55 g/2 oz Cheddar cheese, grated

140 g/5 oz fresh lasagne sheets

salt and pepper

Method

1 Melt half of the butter with the oil in a large saucepan and add the sliced leeks. Stir well and cover with a lid. Cook gently for 10 minutes. Lay the chicken breasts on top of the leeks, season with salt and pepper and cook covered for a further 10–15 minutes, or until the chicken is tender and the juices run clear when a skewer is inserted into the thickest part of the meat. Remove the chicken breasts from the saucepan and set aside. Drain the leeks, reserving the cooking liquid, and set aside.

2 Melt the remaining butter in a small saucepan and add the flour. Cook, stirring to form a paste. Gradually add the reserved leek liquid, stirring well to make a smooth sauce. If the mixture is very thick, add the milk. Stir in half the cheese and check the seasoning. Chop the cooked chicken into very small pieces.

3 Preheat the oven to 200°C/400°F/Gas Mark 6. Lightly grease an ovenproof baking dish and place a sheet of lasagne in the base. Spread a quarter of the cooked leeks on top followed by a quarter of the chopped chicken. Spoon a little sauce over the top. Place another sheet of lasagne on top, pressing down firmly, and repeat the layers of leeks and chicken. Spoon

FILLED & BAKED

ome more sauce on top and then cover with a final lasagne sheet. Use the emaining sauce to cover the surface of the pasta completely. Sprinkle with he remaining cheese and place the dish on a baking sheet. Bake in the preheated oven for 20 minutes, or until golden and bubbling. Leave to cool lightly before serving.

CHICKEN & WILD MUSHROOM CANNELLONI

Serves: 4　　　　**Prep: 25–30 mins**　　　　**Cook: 1 hour 55 mins**

Ingredients

butter, for greasing

2 tbsp olive oil

2 garlic cloves, crushed

1 large onion, finely chopped

225 g/8 oz wild mushrooms, sliced

350 g/12 oz fresh chicken mince

115 g/4 oz prosciutto, diced

150 ml/5 fl oz Marsala wine

200 g/7 oz canned chopped tomatoes

1 tbsp shredded fresh basil leaves

2 tbsp tomato purée

10–12 dried cannelloni tubes

330 ml/10 fl oz béchamel sauce

85 g/3 oz freshly grated Parmesan cheese

salt and pepper

Method

1 Preheat the oven to 190°C/375°F/Gas Mark 5. Lightly grease a large ovenproof dish. Heat the olive oil in a heavy-based frying pan. Add the garlic, onion and mushrooms and cook over a low heat, stirring frequently, for 8–10 minutes. Add the chicken mince and prosciutto and cook, stirring frequently, for 12 minutes, or until browned all over. Stir in the Marsala, tomatoes and their can juices, basil and tomato purée and cook for 4 minutes. Season to taste with salt and pepper, then cover and simmer for 30 minutes. Uncover, stir and simmer for 15 minutes.

2 Bring a large, heavy-based saucepan of lightly salted water to the boil. Add the cannelloni, bring back to the boil and cook for 8–10 minutes or until just tender but still firm to the bite. Using a slotted spoon, transfer to a plate and pat dry.

3 Using a teaspoon, fill the cannelloni tubes with the chicken and mushroom mixture. Transfer them to the dish. Pour the béchamel sauce over them to cover completely and sprinkle with the grated Parmesan cheese.

4 Bake in the preheated oven for 30 minutes, or until golden brown and bubbling. Serve immediately.

FILLED & BAKED

BAKED PASTA WITH MUSHROOMS

Serves: 4   **Prep: 10–15 mins**   **Cook: 25–30 mins**

Ingredients

140 g/5 oz fontina cheese, thinly sliced

660 ml/ 23 fl oz béchamel sauce

6 tbsp butter, plus extra for greasing

350 g/12 oz mixed wild mushrooms, sliced

350 g/12 oz dried tagliatelle

2 egg yolks

salt and pepper

4 tbsp freshly grated romano cheese

mixed salad leaves, to serve

Method

1 Preheat the oven to 200°C/400°F/Gas Mark 6. Stir the fontina cheese into the béchamel sauce and set aside.

2 Melt 2 tablespoons of the butter in a large saucepan. Add the mushrooms and cook over low heat, stirring occasionally, for 10 minutes.

3 Meanwhile, bring a large saucepan of lightly salted water to the boil. Add the pasta, return to the boil and cook for 8–10 minutes, or until tender but still firm to the bite. Drain, return to the pan and add the remaining butter, the egg yolks and about one third of the sauce, then season with salt and pepper. Toss well to mix, then gently stir in the mushrooms.

4 Lightly grease a large, ovenproof dish with butter and spoon in the pasta mixture. Pour over the remaining sauce evenly and sprinkle with the grated romano cheese. Bake in the preheated oven for 15–20 minutes, or until golden brown. Serve immediately with mixed salad leaves.

FILLED & BAKED

MOZZARELLA GNOCCHI

erves: 2   **Prep: 15 mins**   **Cook: 10 mins**

Ingredients

butter, for greasing

g/1 lb potato gnocchi

ml/7 fl oz double cream

5 g/8 oz firm mozzarella
ese, grated or chopped

salt and pepper

Method

1 Preheat the grill to medium and grease
a large baking dish. Cook the gnocchi in a
large saucepan of boiling salted water for
about 3 minutes, or according to the packet
instructions. Drain and put into the prepared
baking dish.

2 Season the cream with salt and pepper and
drizzle over the gnocchi. Scatter over the
cheese and cook under the preheated grill for
a few minutes, or until the top is browned and
bubbling. Serve immediately.

FILLED & BAKED

TURKEY, LEEK & CHEESE CASSEROLE

Serves: 4   **Prep: 20–25 mins**   **Cook: 40–45 mins**

Ingredients

115 g/4 oz dried short macaroni

1 small egg, lightly beaten

2 tbsp butter

4 small leeks, green part included, finely sliced

2 carrots, diced

1 tbsp plain flour

¼ tsp freshly grated nutmeg

250 ml/9 fl oz chicken stock

225 g/8 oz diced cooked turkey or chicken

55 g/2 oz diced ham

3 tbsp chopped fresh flat-leaf parsley

100 g/3½ oz freshly grated Gruyère cheese

salt and pepper

Method

1 Preheat the oven to 180°C/350°F/Gas Mark 4. Bring a large saucepan of lightly salted water boil over a medium heat. Add the pasta, return to the boil and cook for 8–10 minutes, or until tender but still firm to the bite. Drain and return the saucepan. Stir in the egg and a knob of the butter, mixing well. Set aside.

2 Melt the remaining butter in a saucepan over medium heat. Add the leeks and carrots. Cove and cook for 5 minutes, shaking the saucepan occasionally, until just tender.

3 Add the flour and nutmeg. Cook for 1 minute, stirring constantly. Pour in the stock. Bring to the boil, stirring constantly. Stir in the turkey, ham and parsley. Season to taste with salt and pepper.

4 Spread half the turkey mixture over the base of a shallow baking dish. Spread the macaroni ove the turkey. Top with the remaining turkey mixture Sprinkle with the cheese. Bake in the oven for 15–20 minutes. Serve the gratin when the chees is golden and bubbling.

FILLED & BAKED

TURKEY
MANICOTTI

erves: 4　　　　**Prep: 25 mins**　　　　**Cook: 45–50 mins**

Ingredients

1 tbsp olive oil

450 g/1 lb fresh
turkey mince

25 g/8 oz ricotta cheese

55 g/2 oz mozzarella
cheese, grated

0 g/2¼ oz freshly grated
Parmesan cheese

2 eggs, lightly beaten

2 tbsp chopped fresh
flat-leaf parsley

6 dried manicotti

400 g jar tomato
pasta sauce

salt and pepper

Method

1 Preheat the oven to 180°C/350°F/Gas Mark 4.
Heat the oil in a frying pan, add the turkey and
cook over a medium heat, stirring frequently, for
6–8 minutes, until evenly browned. Remove the
pan from the heat and carefully drain off any fat.

2 Mix the ricotta cheese, mozzarella cheese,
40 g/1½ oz of the Parmesan cheese, the eggs
and parsley together in a bowl, season to taste
with salt and pepper and stir in the turkey.

3 Bring a large saucepan of lightly salted water
to the boil. Add the pasta in two batches, bring
back to the boil and cook for 2 minutes. Remove
with a slotted spoon. Divide the turkey mixture
between the manicotti and put them into an
ovenproof dish in a single layer, packing them
closely together.

4 Spoon the tomato sauce evenly over the
manicotti, sprinkle with the remaining Parmesan
cheese and bake for 20–30 minutes, until golden
and bubbling. Serve immediately.

FILLED & BAKED

TURKEY TETRAZZINI

Serves: 4–6　　　**Prep: 25–30 mins**　　　**Cook: 40–45 mins**

Ingredients

3 tbsp olive oil

650 g/1 lb 7 oz turkey breast fillets, diced

115 g/4 oz butter, plus extra for greasing

2 tbsp plain flour

450 ml/16 fl oz chicken stock

dash of hot pepper sauce

1 egg yolk

2 tbsp medium sherry

125 ml/4 fl oz single cream

225 g/8 oz dried tagliatelle

225 g/8 oz mushrooms, sliced

55 g/2 oz freshly grated Parmesan cheese

55 g/2 oz fresh breadcrumbs

salt

Method

1　Heat the oil in a frying pan, add the turkey and cook over a medium heat, stirring frequently, for 8–10 minutes until cooked through. Remove from the heat.

2　Melt half the butter in a saucepan, stir in the flour and cook, stirring constantly, for 1 minute. Remove from the heat and gradually stir in the stock. Return to the heat and bring to the boil, stirring constantly. Boil for 1 minute until thickened and smooth, then stir in the hot pepper sauce, season to taste with salt and remove from the heat.

3　Beat the egg yolk with a fork in a bowl, then beat in 2 tablespoons of the hot sauce. Stir the mixture into the sauce in the pan, then stir in the sherry, cream and turkey. Return the pan to a low heat and heat through, stirring constantly, but do not boil. Remove the pan from the heat.

4　Bring a large saucepan of lightly salted water to the boil. Add the pasta, bring back to the boil and cook for 8–10 minutes, until tender but still firm to the bite. Meanwhile, melt half the remaining butter in a small saucepan, add the mushrooms and cook, stirring occasionally, for 4–5 minutes. Add the mushrooms to the turkey mixture.

FILLED & BAKED

Preheat the grill. Grease a flameproof dish with butter. Drain the pasta. Make alternating layers of the turkey mixture and pasta in the dish. Sprinkle with the grated cheese and breadcrumbs, dot with the remaining butter and cook under the preheated grill until the top is golden and bubbling. Serve immediately.

LASAGNE AL FORNO

Serves: 4 **Prep: 20–25 mins** **Cook: 1 hour 20 mins–1½ hours**

Ingredients

2 tbsp olive oil

55 g/2 oz pancetta, chopped

1 onion, chopped

1 garlic clove, finely chopped

225 g/8 oz fresh beef mince

2 celery sticks, chopped

2 carrots, chopped

pinch of sugar

½ tsp dried oregano

400 g/14 oz canned chopped tomatoes

2 tsp Dijon mustard

450 ml/16 fl oz ready-made cheese sauce

225 g/8 oz dried no pre-cook lasagne sheets

115 g/4 oz freshly grated Parmesan cheese, plus extra for sprinkling

salt and pepper

Method

1 Preheat the oven to 190°C/375°F/Gas Mark 5. Heat the oil in a large, heavy-based saucepan. Add the pancetta and cook over a medium heat, stirring occasionally, for 3 minutes.

2 Add the onion and garlic and cook, stirring occasionally, for 5 minutes, or until soft.

3 Add the beef mince and cook, breaking it up with a wooden spoon, until brown all over with no remaining traces of pink. Stir in the celery and carrots and cook for 5 minutes.

4 Season to taste with salt and pepper. Add the sugar, oregano and tomatoes and their can juices. Bring to the boil, reduce the heat and simmer for 30 minutes.

5 Meanwhile, stir the mustard into the cheese sauce.

6 In a large, rectangular ovenproof dish, make alternate layers of meat sauce, lasagne sheets and Parmesan cheese.

7 Pour the cheese sauce over the layers, covering them completely, and sprinkle with Parmesan cheese.

8 Bake in the preheated oven for 30 minutes, or until golden brown and bubbling. Serve immediately.

FILLED & BAKED

PUMPKIN RAVIOLI

Serves: 4

Prep: 30–35 mins,
plus chilling & drying

Cook: 20 mins

Ingredients

300 g/10½ oz durum wheat
flour, plus extra for dusting

2 eggs

1 tbsp oil

½ tsp salt

1 tsp vinegar

¾ tbsp water

Filling

1 tbsp olive oil

450 g/1 lb pumpkin, cubed

1 shallot, finely diced

125 ml/4 fl oz water,
plus extra for brushing

55 g/2 oz grated Parmesan
cheese

1 egg

1 tbsp finely chopped
fresh flat-leaf parsley

salt and pepper

Method

1 Knead the flour, eggs, oil, salt, vinegar and water into a silky-smooth dough. Wrap the dough in clingfilm and chill in the refrigerator for 1 hour.

2 For the filling, heat the olive oil in a saucepan, add the pumpkin and shallot and sauté until the shallot is translucent. Add the water and cook the pumpkin until the liquid evaporates. Cool slightly, then mix with the cheese, egg, parsley, and salt and pepper.

3 Divide the dough in half. Thinly roll out both pieces. Place small spoonfuls of the pumpkin mixture about 4 cm/1½ inches apart on one sheet of dough. Brush a little water on the space in between. Lay the second sheet of dough on top and press down around each piece of filling. Use a pastry wheel to cut out squares and press the edges together with a fork. Leave the ravioli to dry for 30 minutes, then bring a large saucepan of lightly salted water to the boil. Add the ravioli and cook over a medium heat until tender, but firm to the bite. Remove the ravioli with a slotted spoon and drain well on kitchen paper.

STEAK & PASTA BITES

Serves: 6

Prep: 35–40 mins, plus cooling & chilling

Cook: 1 hour 25 mins–1 hour 35 mins

Ingredients

3 tbsp olive oil

2 onions, chopped

2 garlic cloves, finely chopped

400 g/14 oz canned chopped tomatoes

1 tsp soft light brown sugar

100 ml/3½ fl oz water

12–16 dried cannelloni tubes

450 g/1 lb fresh steak mince

1 tbsp chopped fresh flat-leaf parsley

pinch dried oregano

350 g/12 oz mozzarella cheese, grated

350 g/12 oz ricotta cheese

vegetable oil, for deep-frying

70 g/2½ oz plain flour

2 eggs, lightly beaten

85 g/3 oz fresh breadcrumbs

salt and pepper

Method

1 Heat 2 tablespoons of the olive oil in a saucepan, add half the chopped onions and all the garlic and cook over a low heat for 5 minutes. Stir in the tomatoes, sugar and water and season to taste with salt and pepper. Simmer, stirring occasionally, for 20 minutes. Remove from the heat, ladle 125 ml/4 fl oz into a food processor or blender and process to a coarse purée. Set aside the remaining sauce.

2 Bring a saucepan of lightly salted water to the boil. Add the pasta, bring back to the boil and cook for 5–6 minutes. Drain and set aside on a tea towel.

3 Heat the remaining olive oil in a frying pan, add the remaining onion and cook over a low heat, stirring occasionally, for 5 minutes. Increase the heat to medium, add the mince and cook, stirring frequently, for 5–7 minutes, until brown. Reduce the heat, stir in the herbs and puréed tomato sauce, season to taste with salt and pepper and simmer for 10 minutes. Remove from the heat and leave to cool.

4 Stir the mozzarella cheese and ricotta cheese into the meat mixture, then use to fill the cannelloni tubes. Chill in the freezer for 5 minutes. Heat the vegetable oil to 180–190°C/350–375°F or until a cube of day-old bread browns in

FILLED & BAKED

0 seconds. Cut each cannelloni tube into three pieces. Coat them in the [fl]our, then in the beaten egg and, finally, in breadcrumbs. Add to the hot oil, [i]n batches, and cook for 4–5 minutes, until crisp and golden. Remove and [d]rain on kitchen paper. Reheat the reserved sauce, if necessary, and ladle [o]nto warmed plates. Top with the pasta bites and serve immediately.

PORK & PASTA BAKE

Serves: 4

Prep: 20 mins

Cook: 1 hour 10 mins–1 hour 25 mins

Ingredients

2 tbsp olive oil

1 onion, chopped

1 garlic clove, finely chopped

2 carrots, diced

55 g/2 oz pancetta, chopped

115 g/4 oz mushrooms, chopped

450 g/1 lb minced pork

125 ml/4 fl oz dry white wine

4 tbsp passata

200 g/7 oz canned chopped tomatoes

2 tsp chopped fresh sage or ½ tsp dried sage

225 g/8 oz dried rigatoni

140 g/5 oz mozzarella cheese, diced

4 tbsp freshly grated Parmesan cheese

300 ml/10 fl oz hot béchamel sauce

salt and pepper

Method

1 Preheat the oven to 200°C/400°F/Gas Mark 6. Heat the olive oil in a large, heavy-based frying pan. Add the onion, garlic and carrots and cook over a low heat, stirring occasionally for 5 minutes, or until the onion has softened. Add the pancetta and cook for 5 minutes. Add the chopped mushrooms and cook, stirring occasionally, for an additional 2 minutes. Add the pork and cook, breaking it up with a wooden spoon, until the meat is browned all over. Stir in the wine, passata, chopped tomatoes and the can juices and sage. Season to taste with salt and pepper and bring to the boil, then cover and simmer over a low heat for 25–30 minutes.

2 Meanwhile, bring a large saucepan of lightly salted water to the boil. Add the pasta, bring back to the boil and cook for 8–10 minutes, until tender but still firm to the bite.

3 Spoon the pork mixture into a large ovenproof dish. Stir the mozzarella cheese and half the Parmesan cheese into the béchamel sauce. Drain the pasta and stir the sauce into it, then spoon it over the pork mixture. Sprinkle with the remaining Parmesan cheese and bake in the preheated oven for 25–30 minutes, until golden and bubbling. Serve immediately.

FILLED & BAKED

HAM & PESTO LASAGNE

Serves: 4–6   **Prep: 30 mins**   **Cook: 1 hour 5 mins, plus standing**

Ingredients

40 g/1½ oz butter

3 tbsp plain flour

300 ml/10 fl oz milk

pinch of ground nutmeg

5 tbsp artichoke pesto or basil pesto

350 g/12 oz spinach, rinsed and drained, coarse stalks removed

1 egg, lightly beaten

450 g/1 lb ricotta cheese

250 g/9 oz cooked ham, diced

2 tomatoes, peeled, deseeded and diced

250 g/9 oz dried no pre-cook lasagne sheets

4 tbsp freshly grated Parmesan cheese

salt and pepper

Method

1 Melt the butter in a saucepan, stir in the flour and cook over a low heat, stirring constantly, f 1 minute. Remove from the heat and graduall whisk in the milk. Return to the heat and bring the boil, whisking constantly until thickened ar smooth. Remove from the heat and stir in the nutmeg and pesto.

2 Meanwhile, cook the spinach in just the water clinging to the leaves for 5–10 minutes until wilted. Drain, squeeze out the excess moisture and pat dry, then finely chop.

3 Preheat the oven to 200°C/400°F/Gas Mark 6. Stir the egg into the ricotta cheese and season to taste with salt and pepper. Stir in the spinach ham and tomatoes.

4 Make alternating layers of lasagne, the cheese mixture and the pesto sauce in an ovenproof dish, ending with a layer of lasagne topped wit pesto sauce. Cover the dish with foil and bake the preheated oven for 50 minutes.

5 Remove the dish from the oven, discard the foil and sprinkle the top of the lasagne with the Parmesan cheese. Return to the oven and bake for a further 5 minutes until golden and bubbling Leave to stand for 5 minutes before serving.

FILLED & BAKED

SALMON LASAGNE ROLLS

Serves: 4   **Prep: 25–30 mins**   **Cook: 1 hour 5 mins– 1 hour 10 mins**

Ingredients

8 sheets dried lasagne verde

25 g/1 oz butter

1 onion, sliced

½ red pepper, deseeded and chopped

1 courgette, diced

1 tsp chopped fresh ginger

125 g/4½ oz oyster mushrooms, torn into pieces

225 g/8 oz salmon fillet, skinned and cut into chunks

3 tbsp dry sherry

2 tsp cornflour

vegetable oil, for brushing

3 tbsp plain flour

425 ml/15 fl oz milk

25 g/1 oz finely grated Cheddar cheese

1 tbsp fresh white breadcrumbs

salt and pepper

Method

1 Bring a large saucepan of lightly salted water to the boil. Add the pasta, bring back to the boil and cook for 8–10 minutes, until tender but still firm to the bite. Remove with tongs and drain on a clean tea towel.

2 Melt half the butter in a saucepan. Add the onion and cook over a low heat, stirring occasionally, for 5 minutes, until softened. Add the red pepper, courgette and ginger and cook, stirring occasionally, for 10 minutes. Add the mushrooms and salmon and cook for 2 minutes, then mix together the sherry and cornflour and stir into the pan. Cook for a further 4 minutes, until the fish is opaque and flakes easily. Season to taste with salt and pepper and remove the pan from the heat.

3 Preheat the oven to 200°C/400°F/Gas Mark 6. Brush an ovenproof dish with oil.

4 Melt the remaining butter in another pan. Stir in the flour and cook, stirring constantly, for 2 minutes. Gradually stir in the milk, then cook, stirring constantly, for 10 minutes. Remove the pan from the heat, stir in half the Cheddar cheese and season to taste with salt and pepper.

FILLED & BAKED

Spoon the salmon filling along one of the shorter sides of each sheet of lasagne. Roll up and place in the prepared dish. Pour the sauce over the rolls and sprinkle with the breadcrumbs and remaining cheese. Bake in the preheated oven for 15–20 minutes, until golden and bubbling. Serve immediately.

LASAGNE ALLA MARINARA

Serves: 6　　**Prep: 25 mins**　　**Cook: 45 mins**

Ingredients

15 g/½ oz butter

225 g/8 oz raw prawns, peeled and deveined

450 g/1 lb monkfish fillets, skinned and chopped

225 g/8 oz chestnut mushrooms, chopped

850 ml/24 fl oz béchamel sauce

400 g/14 oz canned chopped tomatoes

1 tbsp chopped fresh chervil

1 tbsp shredded fresh basil

175 g/6 oz dried no pre-cook lasagne

85 g/3 oz freshly grated Parmesan cheese

salt and pepper

Method

1 Preheat the oven to 190°C/375°F/Gas Mark 5. Melt the butter in a large, heavy-based saucepan. Add the prawns and monkfish and cook over a medium heat for 3–5 minutes, or un the prawns change colour. Transfer the prawns t a small heatproof bowl with a perforated spoon Add the mushrooms to the saucepan and cook stirring occasionally, for 5 minutes. Transfer the fish and mushrooms to the bowl.

2 Stir the fish mixture, with any juices, into the béchamel sauce and season to taste with salt and pepper. Layer the tomatoes, chervil, basil, fish mixture and lasagne sheets in a large ovenproof dish, ending with a layer of the fish mixture. Sprinkle evenly with the grated Parmesan cheese.

3 Bake in the preheated oven for 35 minutes, or until golden brown, then serve immediately.

FILLED & BAKED

SICILIAN SPAGHETTI CAKE

Serves: 4   **Prep: 35–40 mins**   **Cook: 1 hour 25 mins–1½ hours**

Ingredients

125 ml/4 fl oz olive oil

2 aubergines, sliced

50 g/12 oz minced beef

1 onion, chopped

2 garlic cloves, chopped finely

2 tbsp tomato purée

400 g/14 oz canned chopped tomatoes

sp Worcestershire sauce

1 tbsp chopped fresh flat-leaf parsley

10 stoned black olives

1 red pepper, deseeded and chopped

75 g/6 oz dried spaghetti

140 g/5 oz freshly grated Parmesan cheese

salt and pepper

Method

1 Preheat the oven to 200°C/400°F/Gas Mark 6. Brush a 20-cm/8-inch loose-based round cake tin with oil and line the bottom with baking paper. Heat half the oil in a frying pan. Add the aubergines in batches, and cook until lightly browned on both sides. Add more oil, as required. Drain the aubergines on kitchen paper, then arrange in overlapping slices to cover the bottom and sides of the tin, reserving a few.

2 Heat the remaining oil in a large saucepan and add the beef, onion and garlic. Cook over a medium heat, breaking up the meat with a spoon, until browned all over. Add the tomato purée, tomatoes, Worcestershire sauce and parsley. Season to taste with salt and pepper and simmer for 10 minutes. Add the olives and red pepper and cook for 10 minutes.

3 Meanwhile, bring a large saucepan of lightly salted water to the boil. Add the pasta, bring back to the boil and cook for 8–10 minutes, until tender but still firm to the bite. Drain and transfer to a bowl. Add the meat sauce and cheese and toss, then spoon into the tin, press down and cover with the remaining aubergine. Bake for 40 minutes. Leave the cake to stand for 5 minutes, then invert onto a plate. Discard the baking paper and serve immediately.

FILLED & BAKED

MACARONI & SEAFOOD BAKE

Serves: 4   **Prep: 20–25 mins**   **Cook: 45–50 mins**

Ingredients

350 g/12 oz dried macaroni

85 g/3 oz butter, plus extra for greasing

2 small fennel bulbs, trimmed and thinly sliced

175 g/6 oz mushrooms, thinly sliced

175 g/6 oz cooked peeled prawns

pinch of cayenne pepper

600 ml/1 pint béchamel sauce

55 g/2 oz freshly grated Parmesan cheese

2 large tomatoes, halved and sliced

olive oil, for brushing

1 tsp dried oregano

salt

Method

1 Preheat the oven to 180°C/350°F/Gas Mark 4. Bring a large saucepan of lightly salted water to the boil. Add the pasta, bring back to the boil and cook for 8–10 minutes, until tender but still firm to the bite.

2 Drain and return to the saucepan. Add 25 g/ 1 oz of the butter to the pasta, cover, shake the saucepan and keep warm.

3 Melt the remaining butter in a separate saucepan. Add the fennel and cook for 3–4 minutes. Stir in the mushrooms and cook for a further 2 minutes. Stir in the prawns, then remove the pan from the heat. Stir the cooked pasta, cayenne pepper and prawn mixture into the béchamel sauce.

4 Grease a large ovenproof dish, then pour the mixture into the dish and spread evenly. Sprinkle over the Parmesan cheese and arrange the tomato slices in a ring around the edge. Brush the tomatoes with oil, then sprinkle over the oregano. Bake in the preheated oven for 25 minutes until golden and bubbling. Serve immediately.

FILLED & BAKED

RAVIOLI WITH CRABMEAT & RICOTTA

Serves: 4

Prep: 35–40 mins, plus resting

Cook: 10 mins

Ingredients

300 g/10½ oz type 00 pasta flour or strong white flour

1 tsp salt

3 eggs, beaten

70 g/2½ oz butter, melted

Filling

175 g/6 oz white crabmeat

175 g/6 oz ricotta cheese

finely grated rind of 1 lemon

pinch of dried chilli flakes

2 tbsp chopped fresh flat-leaf parsley

salt and pepper

Method

1 Sift the flour and salt onto a board or work surface, make a well in the centre and add the eggs.

2 Stir with a fork to gradually incorporate the flour into the liquid to form a dough.

3 Knead for about 5 minutes, until the dough is smooth. Wrap in clingfilm and leave to rest for 20 minutes.

4 For the filling, stir together the crabmeat, ricotta, lemon rind, chilli flakes and parsley. Season to taste with salt and pepper.

5 Roll the dough with a pasta machine or by hand to a thickness of about 3 mm/⅛ inch and cut into 32 x 6-cm/2½-inch squares.

6 Place a spoonful of the filling in the centre of half the squares.

7 Brush the edges with water and place the remaining squares on top, pressing to seal.

8 Bring a saucepan of lightly salted water to the boil. Add the ravioli, bring back to the boil and cook for 3 minutes, or until tender but still firm to the bite. Drain well.

9 Drizzle the melted butter over the ravioli, sprinkle with pepper and serve immediately.

FILLED & BAKED

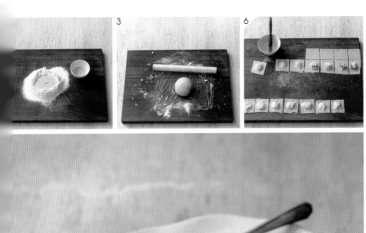

TUNA PASTA BAKE

Serves: 4   **Prep: 25 mins**   **Cook: 40–45 mins, plus standing**

Ingredients

200 g/7 oz dried tagliatelle

25 g/1 oz butter

55 g/2 oz fresh breadcrumbs

400 ml/14 fl oz canned condensed cream of mushroom soup

125 ml/4 fl oz milk

2 celery sticks, chopped

1 red and 1 green pepper, deseeded and chopped

140 g/5 oz mature Cheddar cheese, roughly grated

2 tbsp chopped fresh flat-leaf parsley

200 g/7 oz canned tuna in oil, drained and flaked

salt and pepper

Method

1. Preheat the oven to 200°C/400°F/Gas Mark 6. Bring a large pan of lightly salted water to the boil. Add the pasta and cook for 2 minutes few than specified on the packet instructions.

2. Meanwhile, melt the butter in a small saucepan over a medium heat. Stir in the breadcrumbs, then remove from the heat and reserve.

3. Drain the pasta thoroughly and reserve. Pour the soup into the pasta pan over a medium heat, then stir in the milk, celery, peppers, half the cheese and the parsley. Add the tuna and gently stir in. Season to taste with salt and pepper. Heat just until small bubbles appear around the edge of the mixture – do not boil.

4. Stir the pasta into the pan and use two forks to mix all the ingredients together. Spoon the mixture into an ovenproof dish and spread out. Stir the remaining cheese into the buttered breadcrumbs, then sprinkle over the top of the pasta mixture. Bake in the preheated oven for 20–25 minutes, until golden and bubbling. Leave to stand for 5 minutes before serving.

★ **Variation**

Try using another soup for a more interesting sauce, such as cream of chicken soup.

FILLED & BAKED

INDEX

INDEX

This edition published by Parragon Books Ltd in 2014
LOVE FOOD is an imprint of Parragon Books Ltd

Parragon Books Ltd
Chartist House
15–17 Trim Street
Bath BA1 1HA, UK
www.parragon.com/lovefood

ISBN 978-1-4723-6460-9
Printed in China

Cover photography by Ian Garlick
Introduction by Anne Sheasby

Notes for the Reader
This book uses both metric and imperial measurements. Follow the same units of measurement throughout; do not mix metric and imperial. All spoon measurements are level: teaspoons are assumed to be 5 ml, and tablespoons are assumed to be 15 ml. Unless otherwise stated, milk is assumed to be full fat, eggs and individual vegetables are medium, and pepper is freshly ground black pepper. Unless otherwise stated, all root vegetables should be peeled prior to using.

Garnishes, decorations and serving suggestions are all optional and not necessarily included in the recipe ingredients or method. The times given are an approximate guide only. Preparation times differ according to the techniques used by different people and the cooking times may also vary from those given. Optional ingredients, variations or serving suggestions have not been included in the time calculations.

150
BAKING
recipes

150
CAKE
recipes

150
CHICKEN
recipes

150
CUPCAKE & MUFFIN
recipes

150
FAST & SIMPLE
recipes

150
INDIAN
recipes

150
PASTA
recipes

150
SLOW COOKER
recipes

150
STIR-FRY
recipes

150
STUDENT
recipes

150
TAPAS
recipes

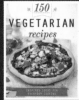
150
VEGETARIAN
recipes